THE
GREEN BERET
BUSHCRAFTING
GUIDE

The Eight Pillars of Survival in Any Situation

BRIAN M. MORRIS
MASTER SERGEANT (RETIRED), UNITED STATES ARMY SPECIAL FORCES

T0006363

Skyhorse Publishing

Copyright © 2023 by Brian M. Morris
Photography © 2023 by Getty Images unless otherwise noted

Skyhorse Publishing books may be purchased in bulk at special discounts for sales promotion, corporate gifts, fund-raising, or educational purposes. Special editions can also be created to specifications. For details, contact the Special Sales Department, Skyhorse Publishing, 307 West 36th Street, 11th Floor, New York, NY 10018 or info@skyhorsepublishing.com.

Skyhorse® and Skyhorse Publishing® are registered trademarks of Skyhorse Publishing, Inc.®, a Delaware corporation.

Visit our website at www.skyhorsepublishing.com.
10 9 8 7 6 5 4 3 2 1

Library of Congress Cataloging-in-Publication Data is available on file.

Cover design by Kai Texel
Cover photos by Getty Images

Print ISBN: 978-1-5107-7145-1
Ebook ISBN: 978-1-5107-7146-8

Printed in China

"Give me six hours to chop down a tree and I will spend the first four sharpening the axe."
—Abraham Lincoln

Table of Contents

(every-day carry) bag. An EDC bag is nothing more than a sack containing a group of items meant to assist you in getting back to safety in the event that you find yourself in an emergency scenario. The idea is that you should keep these items on your person or in your vehicle at all times, so that if you ever do find yourself in a survival situation, you will have maximized your chances for surviving the ordeal and returning home safely. There is a plethora of backpacks on the market today and it's hard to say which one is best, but you want to look for a pack that is both comfortable to carry for long distances and that is made with thick, strong materials with reinforced stitching that will not come apart when you need it most. Size will vary on how much you need to carry with you in the environment that you are in to be able to survive and make your way back to safety.

EDC BAG CONTENTS

- Concealed carry pistol with additional magazine (refer to state law for permit requirements)
- Keys with lanyard or flotation device
- Less-than-lethal device (taser, stun gun, or mace)
- Survival kit, individual
- Flashlight, tactical
- Multi-tool
- Watch
- Cell phone (with charger cable, plug, spare battery pack)
- Wallet with CCW permit, ID, credit card, and cash
- Medical mask
- Food (minimum of 3 meals and several energy bars)
- Water (2 quarts)
- Pry bar
- Bolt cutters
- Knife (full tang)
- First aid kit
- Space blanket
- AM/FM/shortwave emergency radio, small
- Walking shoes and hiking socks (seasonal)
- Change of clothing (outdoor/rugged/seasonally oriented) with gloves and hat
- Rain poncho
- Sunglasses
- Goggles

- Glass/window punch
- Bandana
- Charging devices (battery and solar)
- Paper map (local/detailed and large-scale, showing clear routes back to your home)
- GPS device (if not on smartphone)
- PLB (personal locator beacon)
- 550 cord
- Carabiner

PACE PLAN

PACE (Primary, Alternate, Contingency, Emergency) is an acronym commonly used by Green Berets as a tool to memorize a series of plans that help ensure they have multiple survival options to choose from in an emergency situation. Remember, emergency situations can be highly fluid and knowing when to stop what you are doing and refocus on something completely different can be a difficult thing to do. People run into problems in the wilderness when signs to change course are ignored. You can apply a PACE Plan in order to maximize your chances of survival no matter what the situation.

Take a look at the following PACE Plan and tailor a plan that fits your own personal level of preparedness. **Note:** This PACE Plan is based off the assumption that the survivor is dressed appropriately for the outside weather conditions and that they have their EDC (every-day carry) bag with them.

FOOD

- **P:** 6 (5,000-calorie) freeze-dried meals with my EDC bag
- **A:** SDS Imports Lynx LH-12 Gauge Shotgun and US Survival AR-7 .22 LR Rifle
- **C:** 6 (500-calorie) power bars with my EDC bag
- **E:** Field expedient (survival knife and survival kit: i.e., hunt, trap/snare, fish, gather)

WATER

- **P:** 1 (3-quart) water bladder drinking system and 2 (2-quart) Nalgene bottles
- **A:** Water filtration system (such as LifeStraw)
- **C:** Alternate purification methods (i.e., UV, iodine, chlorine)
- **E:** Field expedient method (i.e., boil; field expedient filter, rainwater catch)

SHELTER

- **P:** Clothing/gear
- **A:** Tent/poncho shelter
- **C:** Mylar blanket/survival shelter
- **E:** Field expedient method (i.e., debris hut, swamp bed, snow cave, etc.)

SECURITY

- **P:** SDS Imports Lynx LH-12 Gauge Shotgun and US Survival AR-7 .22 LR Rifle
- **A:** Beretta PX4 Storm Type F 9mm Sub-Compact Centerfire Pistol
- **C:** Taser/stun gun and mace/pepper spray (bear spray)
- **E:** 7" Full Tang Tanto Survival Knife, hands, and brain

COMMUNICATIONS

- **P:** Cell phone/satellite phone
- **A:** Walkie-talkie
- **C:** Road flares, smoke grenades, fireworks, etc.
- **E:** PLB (Personal Locator Beacon), survival radio and field expedient signaling: i.e., GTAS (Ground To Air Signals) such as smoke signals, mirror, ground symbols/panels, etc.

HEALTH AND FIRST AID

- **P:** IFAK (Individual First Aid Kit)
- **A:** Prescribed medications and preventive medicine procedures adhered to
- **C:** Chemical/biological protective mask and N95 mask
- **E:** Field expedient medicine (e.g., medicinal use of plants, home remedies, wilderness medicine techniques)

LAND NAVIGATION

- **P:** GPS
- **A:** 1:50,000-scale map or other comparable hiking map or road atlas, lensatic compass, protractor, pace beads, map pen
- **C:** Survival button compass
- **E:** Field expedient direction, finding techniques

FIRECRAFT

- **P:** Lighter
- **A:** Road flare
- **C:** Solid fuel tabs, magnesium bar, other commercial incendiaries
- **E:** Field expedient fire-starting techniques (friction fire, battery, magnifier, fire piston, etc.—all items should be in firecraft kit in EDC bag)

PACE PLAN

FOOD
P:

A:

C:

E:

WATER
P:

A:

C:

E:

SHELTER
P:

A:

C:

E:

SECURITY
P:

A:

C:

E:

COMMUNICATIONS
P:

A:

C:

E:

HEALTH AND FIRST AID

P:

A:

C:

E:

LAND NAVIGATION

P:

A:

C:

E:

FIRECRAFT

P:

A:

C:

E:

S.U.R.V.I.V.A.L

S.U.R.V.I.V.A.L is an acronym taught at the Special Forces as well as other survival schools to help troops prioritize and organize themselves should they find themselves cut off from anyone who could help them and need to survive in the wilderness and orchestrate or facilitate rescue either by helping themselves to be found or by navigating their way back to safety, living off the land until they do. Use the keyword S.U.R.V.I.V.A.L as soon as you identify that you are in a real-world survival situation. Each letter in the word S.U.R.V.I.V.A.L stands for a different rule.

- **S: Size up the situation.** Inventory your equipment. Consider who is with you, and your familiarity with the environment you are in.
- **U: Undue haste makes waste.** You don't want to make hasty decisions in a survival situation. Hasty decisions are often careless decisions and carelessness in a survival scenario can be deadly. Take it slow and think out every move you make out.
- **R: Remember where you are.** One of your first priorities in a survival situation is to know your location on the ground. If you don't know where you are, it is extremely difficult to understand where you are going. If you want to have any chance of moving to safety

or facilitating your rescue, the worst thing you can do is to wander aimlessly through the wilderness.

- **V: Vanquish fear and panic.** Fear is nature's way of telling you to stay alert and pay attention to your surroundings. At healthy levels fear can be a good thing. It is when you allow fear to debilitate your actions that it becomes panic. Panic is the worst possible thing you can do in a survival scenario. The main reason people panic is fear of the unknown. The best way to combat and control your fear is to have the courage to face it and recognize it. Once you understand your fear, you will be able to better control it and not let it develop into panic.
- **I: Improvise.** In a survival situation, you may have very few resources to use to help you survive the situation that you are in. It is imperative that you look around you and use every tool and resource that you have at your disposal for as many different purposes as you can think of. Don't let anything go to waste.
- **V: Value living.** Never give up! Facing a survival scenario may be the hardest thing you have ever done as well as the most physically and mentally demanding situation that you have ever found yourself in. If you don't value your own life enough to drive forward through adversity, then there is a real possibility that you will die before effecting self-recovery or being rescued.
- **A: Act like the natives.** Look around you. No matter what environment you are in there are native people, animals, and plants that are not only surviving but thriving. If you want to survive, you should pay particular attention to how they find food, water, and shelter, and how they adapt to their environments in order to survive.
- **L: Live by your wits (but for now, learn basic skills).** As far as living by your wits, all humans have a "sixth sense," a little voice inside our heads that alerts us to danger. The key is to learn to listen to that little voice instead of suppressing it like so many of us do. Learn basic survival skills. Trying to learn bushcraft skills after you have found yourself in a survival scenario is not the way to go about doing things. You should read books, watch videos, take classes, and most of all, get out into the great outdoors and practice your bushcraft survival skills to the point where your survival instincts and knowledge base is ready to tackle any survival situation or scenario that life has to throw at you!

PERSONAL SURVIVAL KITS

In preparing your survival kit, select items you can use for more than one purpose. If you have two items that serve the same function, pick the one you can use for another function. Do not duplicate items, as this increases your kit's size and weight. Your survival kit should be small enough to be carried on your person so that even if separated from your every-day carry bag you will still have the most essential items to help you survive.

Your survival kit need not be elaborate. You need only functional items and a case to hold them. For the case, you might want to use a Band-Aid box, a first aid case, an ammunition pouch, or another suitable case. This case should be:
- Water repellent or waterproof
- Easy to carry or attach to your body
- Suitable to accept various sized components
- Durable

In your survival kit, you should have:
- First aid items
- Water purification tablets or drops
- Fire starting equipment

- Signaling items
- Food procurement items
- Shelter items

Some examples of these items are:
- Lighter, metal match, waterproof matches
- Snare wire
- Signaling mirror
- Wrist compass
- Fish and snare line
- Fishhooks
- Candle
- Small hand lens
- Oxytetracycline tablets (diarrhea or infection)
- Water purification tablets
- Solar blanket
- Surgical blades
- Butterfly sutures
- Condoms for water storage
- Chapstick
- Needle and thread
- Knife
- Wire hand saw

VEHICLE PREPAREDNESS CHECKLIST

There have been too many wilderness survival scenarios that started out as a simple road trip but went bad somewhere along the way because of natural circumstances such as inclement weather and poor preparation like not having additional food, water, clothing, or gear in the vehicle, poor planning,  getting lost, or tough luck. The best way to make sure your next road trip doesn't make the 5 o'clock news is to never travel on an extended road trip, particularly through unknown or sparsely populated areas, without first dedicating time to prepare yourself and your vehicle for emergencies. If you follow this vehicle preparedness checklist you will greatly improve your chances of survival if you ever find yourself stranded and in need of rescue:

- Cell phone (with vehicle charger and stand-alone back-up power charger)
- CB radio
- Police scanner
- Walkie-talkies
- AM/FM/shortwave emergency radio
- Flashlights and extra batteries
- Emergency strobe
- Spotlight (either handheld or vehicle mounted)
- Emergency signal panel
- Road flares
- Reflective triangle
- Jumper cables
- Fix-a-Flat
- Emergency jump starter
- Bag of sand
- Small air compressor
- Tow strap (or tow cable)
- Spare tire
- Tire jack with lug wrench
- Tire traction straps (or chains)
- Spare parts: belts, hoses, fuses, fluids
- Folding shovel
- Ice scraper
- Local road maps
- First aid kit (comprehensive)
- 1 non-perishable meal per person in your party
- 1 gallon of water per person in your party
- 1 blanket (wool) per person in your party
- 1 space blanket per person in your party
- Warm clothes, gloves, hat, sturdy boots, and jacket per person in your party
- Extra baby formula and diapers if you have a small child
- Spare gas cans (carry enough fuel to get you to your next refuel location, taking into consideration vehicle weight when loaded down and possible detours)

ADDITIONAL ITEMS TO CONSIDER
- Assorted hand tools according to your needs

- EDC bag (one per person in your party)
- Bushcraft knife
- Survival kit (individual)
- Flashlights and hands-free lights and batteries
- GPS, compass, maps, protractor, marking pens, pace count beads
- Binoculars
- Fire-starting kit
- Firearm with ammunition
- _____
- _____
- _____

Always top off the fuel tank before leaving on an excursion. Don't wait until your gauge hits empty; better to stop and fill up when the tank is half full. Also, keep your vehicle well maintained and always check the tires to ensure that they are operable and properly inflated.

GENERAL CLOTHING CHOICES FOR THE OUTDOORS

The wilderness is as dangerous as it is beautiful and could easily kill the unprepared or ill-equipped person. Even the most modern clothing and gear if used or cared for improperly will not help you. One of the reasons that the United States Army Special Forces have such a rich history of success in combat is not because they are supermen; it is because they spend an unbelievable amount of time training for, equipping, and preparing for not only  their mission but also for every conceivable contingency plan if things go south. You can put that same mentality to work for you. Shelter is one of the essential elements of life and clothing is the first line of defense in sheltering your body from the elements. Having the proper clothing in certain environments can easily make the difference between life and death. You need to take care of your clothing so that in turn it will be able to best take care of you.

This section will help guide you through the proper selection and use of clothing and personal protective gear and hopefully it will give you a greater chance to survive and thrive in in any environment you may find yourself in. One caveat would be that your vehicle does not offer you immunity to the dangers and risks of being in the wilderness, so having the right clothing and gear extends to when you travel in a vehicle from point A to point B. More than a few survival situations start from a broken-down or stuck vehicle. Remember Murphy's Law, anything that can go wrong will go wrong at the absolute most inopportune time, so the best way to stay alive is to stay two steps ahead of Murphy and always wear the appropriate clothing for the climate zone and weather conditions you are going into, and always bring your EDC bag with you whenever feasible.

SHIRTS

Contrary to popular belief, wearing a T-shirt or not wearing a shirt at all in high heat situations when the sun is blaring down on you is not always the best way to cool your body and protect yourself from the harmful rays of the sun. In areas of high heat and low humidity, look for shirts with long sleeves and light colors. If you need an undergarment to wear under your shirt, look for one that will not cause you to rash in the high

heat and that provides your body with good ventilation. As for fabrics to use in hot weather environments, there are several. Cotton is one of those fabrics that most people would suggest wearing in the heat because it soaks up all the perspiration from your body, allowing it to evaporate slowly, and allows the heat to be wicked away from your skin, but one of the problems with cotton is that it tends to bunch up and cause chafing when it gets wet. While cotton is not a bad choice, there are other options out there. There have been some amazing advances in fabric technology as a byproduct of almost two decades of continuous wars being fought by our military in very extreme high- and low-temperature environments. Polyester-based knits do an excellent job at letting moisture from your sweat evaporate quite quickly which will help to keep you much cooler when you are moving and will then dry quickly when you stop. There are even some wool fabrics out there that will help keep you cool from the summer heat. Merino wool, for instance, has small "pockets" woven into the fabric that absorb water, allowing it to seep out slowly, which helps greatly in keeping your body temperature down. A bonus of wool is that it does not absorb body odor, which is an advantage when hunting prey who have a keen sense of smell.

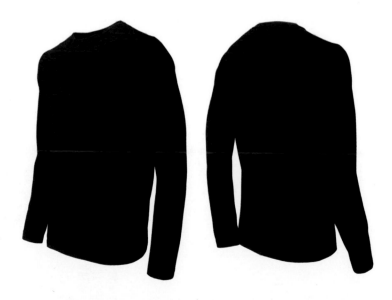

PANTS

Follow the same rules as shirts by selecting fabrics that are lightweight, loose-fitting, and have light colors. Look for pants that perform multifunctions such as the ability to transform into shorts. Pants that have multiple pockets with Velcro or zipper flaps are an added bonus because they give you have a place to secure your gear and valuables.

HIKING BOOTS AND CAMP SHOES

Hiking boots are not an easy thing to choose, as it is almost impossible to find a single pair of shoes that will do a good job at every activity. What you want to do is look for a high-cut, full-grain leather hiking boot to offer you maximum ankle support and durability when traveling on foot in the wilderness. For short walks around your

© Christopher Goldblatt

campsite, you can get a second pair of boots with a low- or mid-cut for adequate but not superior ankle support and made from a more breathable synthetic or leather-synthetic mix. You may also want to consider a third pair of shoes designed specifically for protecting your feet in the water if you expect to be walking across water obstacles, fording rivers, or searching for food in streams and creeks. A good shoe for this is either a well-made pair of waterproof sandals or a good pair of water shoes.

Sizing your shoes: Shoes are without a doubt one of the most important pieces of clothing and equipment that you can have when you are spending time in the outdoors and putting a considerable amount of mileage on your feet. A good pair of shoes can make the difference between an enjoyable experience and a nightmare scenario where every step brings excruciating pain. A survival situation only compounds the need for a pair of shoes that fit correctly and are designed to handle any abuse that you put on them without failure. When searching for the right pair of outdoor shoes, fit is everything. To find the right fit, you first want to ensure that the "last," the wooden foot that the manufacturer chooses to build the shoe around, is a match for your individual foot size. If you try on a shoe and your foot either has way too much room left to move around in the shoe or your foot seems to swell over the shape of the bottom of the shoe, the last is most likely not a good fit for you. What you want is a shoe that is snug around your foot with a hiking sock on. If you are buying boots and your feet are not swollen from walking, wear a thicker pair of socks to represent your foot size after you have been walking on them for some time. If you can't find a pair of shoes that seem to fit the way you want them to, consider seeing your podiatrist to get custom-made orthotics. Blisters are one of the biggest problems that the wrong shoes and socks can cause. Blisters are caused by friction between your foot and your boot or sock.

Socks: The same factors apply to socks regardless of the temperature. That said, you don't have to worry so much about the insulating qualities of your socks in the summertime, and you want a sock that allows your feet to sweat and wicks away any remaining moisture so that your feet remain dry.

An old Green Beret trick for protecting the feet is to use pantyhose as a thin first layer as part of a two-sock system. It will allow friction to occur between the sock and the pantyhose instead of the sock and the skin.

SUNGLASSES

While the range of sunglasses quality and price is quite large, the only factor that really matters when looking for a good pair of sunglasses is if they block 100 percent of UV rays from the sun. When you see the word "polarization" on your sunglasses, it simply means that the glasses are designed in such a way that they can reduce the amount of glare that comes off reflective surfaces such as water or pavement.

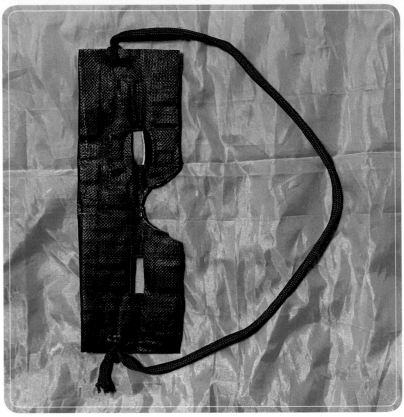

© Brian Morris

HATS

Cooling technology has actually come a long way and there are now several fabrics on the market that provide evaporative cooling technology into their hats and other garments that assist in keeping the body temperature down.

GLOVES

The idea behind finding the perfect pair of gloves seems simple but in reality you may need to have several different pairs of gloves to wear when doing different activities. An easy way to classify what gloves you need for the job is to "weigh" the following areas and then determine which gloves are the best for you:

- Durability and protection
- Fit and dexterity
- Comfort

You may find it difficult to find one single set of gloves that meet all of the above-mentioned criteria equally. For instance, while a form fitting pair of leather gloves will provide excellent protection from friction and labor-intensive work, they will not do a great job at keeping your fingers warm in the winter. Again, you may need to get either several pairs of gloves or look for a glove "system" that can be modified to meet several criteria by simply switching out system components for different activities.

WET WEATHER CONSIDERATIONS

RAIN GEAR

Rain gear is always a good thing to have with you, whether you are wearing it out into the wilderness or simply keeping it in the trunk of your car. While rain gear comes in many forms and configurations, from two-piece to jumpsuit to poncho, they all have one thing in common: they provide a nonporous waterproof surface that protects you from the rain, snow, ice, and wind. We are often confused when searching for rain gear between the terms "waterproof" and "water-resistant." While water-resistant will help to keep you dry, it is not waterproof and it will eventually succumb to heavy rain, leaving you soaked through. The reason people choose water-resistant over waterproof is that waterproof materials will not allow your body to wick off perspiration when you are moving and there is the possibility that you could experience discomfort or even cold injury if you don't find another way to dry off or keep warm. That said, if you are in a stationary or "static" position where activity is limited, it is smart to have a set of waterproof rain gear to put on in order to keep you dry when the rain comes down. Waterproof ponchos have the added benefit of making great shelter tops when getting yourself out of the elements is desired. Don't forget the importance of keeping your feet dry and warm. Consider jungle boots in warmer climates or a good insulated waterproof boot in colder climates.

COLD WEATHER CONSIDERATIONS

Before we talk about cold weather clothing selection, let's first discuss the different types of cold weather you may encounter. Cold weather can be subcategorized as:

- Wet cold
- Dry cold
- Intense cold
- Extreme cold

Often you will encounter several of these conditions, requiring you to be prepared for multiple cold weather conditions.

WET COLD

Wet-cold conditions occur when temperatures are near freezing and variations in the day and night temperatures cause alternate freezing and thawing. Wet-cold temperature ranges from 20°F to 40°F (-7°C to 4°C), not including the windchill. These conditions are often accompanied by wet snow and rain. During these types of weather scenarios, you should look for clothing that has a waterproof, wind-resistant outer layer and an inner layer with sufficient insulation to provide protection down to 20°F (-7°C).

DRY COLD

Dry-cold conditions occur when average temperatures are lower than 20°F (-7°C), the ground is usually frozen, and the snow is dry. Temperatures range from -5°F to 20°F (-21°C to -7°C) for dry cold, not including windchill. Insulating layers must protect to -5°F (-21°C). A water- and wind-resistant outer layer must protect these layers. A good way to check the consistency of snow is to try to make a snowball. If you cannot, then you know the snow is very dry. The wetter snow is, the easier it is to make a snowball.

INTENSE COLD
Intense-cold temperature ranges from -5°F to -25°F (-21° C to -32°C), not including windchill. Substantial insulating layers are required. All tasks and movement are severely slowed down. Extreme care must be taken to avoid environmental casualties.

EXTREME COLD
Extreme-cold temperatures are -26°F (-32°C) and below, not including windchill. This is the most dangerous subcategory of cold weather and you must be extremely careful when exposing yourself and your gear to these kinds of temperatures. You can expect unprotected gear to fail under these conditions, and bodily exposure for any length of time without protection can be fatal.

COMBATTING THE COLD
Now that you know the types of cold weather conditions you may experience, let's discuss some facts that will allow you to better combat the cold.

COOLING POWER OF WIND EXPRESSED AS "EQUIVALENT CHILL TEMPERATURE"

WIND SPEED		TEMPERATURE (DEGREES C)																				
CALM	CALM	4	2	-1	-4	-7	-9	-12	-15	-18	-21	-23	-26	-29	-32	-34	-37	-40	-43	-46	-48	-51
KNOTS	KPH	EQUIVALENT CHILL TEMPERATURE																				
4	8	2	-1	-4	-7	-9	-12	-15	-18	-21	-23	-26	-29	-32	-34	-37	-40	-43	-46	-48	-54	-57
9	16	-1	-7	-9	-12	-15	-18	-23	-26	-29	-32	-37	-40	-43	-46	-51	-54	-57	-59	-62	-68	-71
13	24	-4	-9	-12	-18	-21	-23	-29	-32	-34	-40	-43	-46	-51	-54	-57	-62	-65	-68	-73	-76	-79
17	32	-7	-12	-15	-18	-23	-26	-32	-34	-37	-43	-46	-51	-54	-59	-62	-65	-71	-73	-79	-82	-84
22	40	-9	-12	-18	-21	-26	-29	-34	-37	-43	-46	-51	-54	-59	-62	-68	-71	-76	-79	-84	-87	-93
26	48	-12	-15	-18	-23	-29	-32	-34	-40	-46	-48	-54	-57	-62	-65	-71	-73	-79	-82	-87	-90	-96
30	56	-12	-15	-21	-23	-29	-34	-37	-40	-46	-51	-54	-59	-62	-68	-73	-76	-82	-84	-90	-93	-98
35	64	-12	-18	-21	-26	-29	-34	-37	-43	-48	-51	-57	-59	-65	-71	-73	-79	-82	-87	-90	-96	-101
(Higher winds have little additional effects)		LITTLE DANGER					INCREASING DANGER (Flesh may freeze within 1 minute)						GREAT DANGER (Flesh may freeze within 30 seconds)									

DANGER OF FREEZING EXPOSED FLESH FOR PROPERLY CLOTHED PERSONS

© US Army

To help remember some of the basic principles of how to wear clothing when the temperature is low you can use the acronym "COLD":

C: Keep clothing clean
Clothing keeps you warm by trapping warm air against your body and in the pores of the clothing itself. However, if these pores are filled with dirt, sweat, or other grime, it will not be able to do its job as efficiently.

O: Avoid overheating
Allowing just enough clothes and body activity to keep you cool and the environment to cool you down will keep your clothes from getting sweaty and dirty, and therefore be more effective. Overheating can also cause problems, and not with just your clothes. Several cold weather injuries can be caused by dehydration, hyperthermia, and hypothermia.

L: Loose and layered
You want to keep your clothes loose for comfort. If clothing is too tight it will constrict the flow of blood to your extremities, thereby causing limb(s)

to get cold. Warm air can be trapped between your body and clothes, often keeping you warmer than the clothing itself. The more layers, the more air can be trapped. Several thin layers of clothing working together will work better than one thick layer working alone.

D: Keep clothing dry
You should put on a shell/protective layer when walking through sleet or wet snow. In addition, it helps to take a layer off when you start sweating because once your clothes are wet, the water or sweat starts to evaporate, drawing off warmth with it.

LAYERING

A good technique for wearing clothing in cold weather is to utilize a three-layered approach with a vapor transmission (moisture-wicking) layer, insulating layer, and protective outer layer.

Vapor transmission layer: Better called a "sweat transfer layer," this is a hydrophobic layer that does not absorb your perspiration. This layer draws moisture away from the skin to keep you dry and warm. Significant progress has been made with synthetics, such as polypropylene, which draw water away from the body, but stay dry.
Insulating layer: This can be one layer or several layers that hold(s) the warm air around your body. Preferably,

© Brian Morris

it is lightweight, very compressible, and fast drying. Inner layers are adjusted according to preference, metabolism, and weather conditions to avoid over-heating when on the move and cold weather injury when not. Take off insulating layers during movement to keep them dry and put back on upon stopping. Add or remove insulating layers as needed to avoid sweating and/or chills.

Protective layer: This protects the insulating layer(s) from getting wet or dirty. In cold-wet environments, it should be made of a windproof/water-proof material.

CLOTHING CONSIDERATIONS FOR COLD WEATHER

COLD/WET WEATHER FOOTWEAR

When venturing out into the cold, one of the most critical items of gear that you can have is proper footwear. You should consider having several sets of boots: one pair with a vapor barrier to keep the heat in and the moisture out for when you are static and not travel-ing very far on foot or for extreme cold conditions where exposure to the tem-perature could cause frostbite, and one pair designed for long foot movement that provides both warmth and com-fort as well as support and flexibility.

SNOWSHOES, CRAMPONS, ICE CLEATS, AND OTHER FOOT TRACTION DEVICES

If you know you are going to be trav-eling over snow and ice you should also consider bringing snowshoes, crampons, ice cleats, and other foot traction devices. In extreme condi-tions you will want every advantage you can get if you have to travel across icy and snow-covered terrain; particularly if you are in a survival situation.

LEG GAITERS

Leg gaiters are worn in conjunction with boots to provide protection from getting snow or debris into the boot itself. You can purchase or construct thicker gaiters designed to lower the risk of being bitten by a snake in warmer climate zones/seasons.

GLOVES (COLD WEATHER)

When you are outside in extreme cold situations the three parts of your body most susceptible to frostbite are your fingers, toes, and face. To protect your hands, you want a pair of gloves that will provide both insulation and airflow. Consider mitten shells with insulated inserts in extreme cold environments. Gloves should have a wind- and waterproof outer layer and an insulated liner or set of inserts.

COLD WEATHER HATS

You lose the majority of your body heat from your head, and your face is extremely vulnerable to cold weather injury, so it is very important to protect your head and face from extreme cold situations. There are many types of hats out there, but I recommend wearing a multipurpose hat that can protect your head from heat loss with earflaps to unsnap to protect the sides and back of your head as well. In extreme cold scenarios consider wearing a neck and face gaiter or military-style insulated balaclava as well as a pair of snow goggles to completely insulate and protect your entire face.

COLD WEATHER SUNGLASSES/GOGGLES

You can purchase sunglasses that are specifically designed for use in areas where snow is a prominent part of the outdoor landscape. Snow blindness is a very real problem in high-altitude, snow-covered terrain. Even on overcast days, the possibility exists for snow blindness

to develop. Always use sunglasses with side shields that are designed to filter out ultraviolet rays. If you do not have sunglasses, you can make a pair to protect you from snow blindness by cutting two slits out of cardboard where your eyes would be and then fashioning a makeshift strap to hold them on.

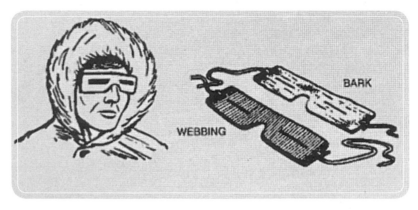

© US Army

© Brian Morris

Tips to Keep Warm

- A good tip for keeping your fingers warm when using gloves is to pull your fingers out of their compartments, keeping them In the gloves, and make a fist. Your warm palm surrounding the fingers will warm them up.
- Put all clothing for the morning inside of your sleeping bag and it will be warm when you wake up.
- You heat your sleeping bag, not the other way around. Therefore, just before going to sleep, eat something high in carbohydrates to give your body fuel to burn during through the night.
- Fill your canteens and Camelbaks® with warm water and keep them in your sleeping bag with you at night. The warm water will help to keep you warm at night and your body heat will keep the canteens from freezing so that you will have water for hygiene, cooking, and drinking when you wake up
- If you find yourself unprepared for whatever climate you find yourself in, all is not lost! Use your creativity and ingenuity to construct your own protective clothing from whatever resources you can find around you. The foam in seat cushions makes for excellent insulatIon. Field expedient snowshoes can be easily constructed by strapping pine bows to your feet. Insulating materials can be wrapped and tied around your extremIties to keep them warm. You can even stuff dry leaves and pine needles into your existing clothing to keep you warm. Your imagination truly is your only limit!

ADDITIONAL OUTDOOR GEAR

TENT
A well-made four-seasons tent with reinforced zippers and seams is ideal for prolonged outdoor survival.

SLEEPING BAG
Ensure that you have a sleeping bag appropriately rated to the temperature zone you are in. If it never drops below 50°F, you do not need a subzero rated sleeping bag. If temperatures are known to drop, you must ensure the sleeping bag you have is rated to the appropriate temperature. If you are in a situation where you need to improvise, you can add insulating layers to the outside and inside of your bag with whatever materials are available to you.

HAMMOCK

Hammocks roll up small and make for an excellent sleeping platform. Many hammocks come with a rain fly and bug net incorporated into them, mak-  ing them a complete shelter system that can keep you off of the ground and away from harmful insects and other unwanted visitors.

FLASHLIGHT

Having a good flashlight is super important and can save you from making your situation worse in many cases. Consider a flashlight that runs on batteries that can be recharged during daylight hours. Tape extra batteries to the outside of your flashlight or to the head harness on your headlamp. The human eye when properly adjusted to the nighttime environment can actually see quite well when traveling through open terrain, so use your flashlight only for map checks or to navigate through danger.

© Brian Morris

SHOVEL

A good folding shovel is an outstanding piece of equipment to have in an emergency, as it can provide many different functions, from digging a trench around your sleeping area to keep out water, to chopping wood for a fire, to digging a cat hole to defecate in. A shovel can even be used as a weapon for hunting or defense.

SURVIVAL KNIFE

Right next to a lighter, a survival knife is arguably one of the most important tools that you can have with you in the wilderness. See more about knife selection on page 100.

COMPASS

A compass is a magnetometer used for orientation and navigation. It shows direction relative to cardinal directions of north, south, east, and west. The circumference of a compass is generally represented by a 360-degree circle with each tick mark on the compass ring representing 1 degree. Some compasses show an even greater accuracy with a 6400-mil ring.

WATER FILTRATION STRAW

Personal water filtration straws are an outstanding way to ensure that you will always have a fast and easy way to decontaminate the bacteria that is often present in water, and it eliminates the need to first boil water before drinking it. Many of the filtration straws available today have proven to protect against 99.999999% of

© AnnMarie Mello-Morris

bacteria (including E. coli and salmonella), parasites (including giardia and cryptosporidium), microplastics, dirt, sand, and cloudiness. Additionally, one filtration straw can filter upward of four thousand gallons of water, enough to keep one person alive for five years.

FOOD

If you are lucky enough to have your EDC pack with you when you find yourself in a survival scenario, you should then have access to an emergency food source. Most of the survival foods available today are packed with carbohydrates to offer the survivor the energy boost that could give them the will and drive to persevere and get themselves through a situation that may have seemed otherwise impossible.

> EDC bags, bug-out bags, 72-hour packs, 3-day assault packs . . . these are all just versions of what Green Berets have been carrying for years and are, at their root, simply a "go bag" that has all of the essentials you need when it's time to get up and go!

INDIVIDUAL FIRST AID KIT (IFAK)

Any time you are going on a planned excursion into the wilderness, having a first aid kit with you is absolutely essential and could easily save your life. According to the US Army, IFAKs should contain at a bare minimum:

- Burn dressing
- Combat (hemostatic) gauze
- Medical gloves
- Ibuprofen
- Israeli dressings
- Pen light
- Permanent marker
- Pressure dressings
- Tourniquet
- Trauma shears
- Vented chest seal

MAP

Most people who venture out on a day hike assume they do not need a map and GPS so long as they keep on the trails and the trails are clearly marked. The fact is that every year scores of hikers find themselves disoriented and become lost. State park and reserve maps can be purchased in stores, online, or by request from the National Park Service. 1:50,000-scale maps or maps of any size can be purchased online and you can get them for virtually every square kilometer on earth. Having a map of the area you are venturing into is very smart and can save you from making some huge mistakes and can maybe even save your life.

Green Berets have a saying, "Map work *before* foot work," that stresses the importance of doing a thorough map reconnaissance and having a good idea of what your chosen route should look like before you start walking. This way you will know what type of terrain you will be walking on and can plan for any special gear, equipment, or clothing you may need.

GRID POSITIONING SYSTEM (GPS)

Keeping a GPS with you can mitigate the chances of a day hike needlessly turning into a survival scenario. They are a great tool to mark waypoints, plan routes, and a plethora of other things. That said, a GPS should *never* replace the need to understand basic orienteering, map reading, and land navigation skills. Depending on a GPS or any electronic device to safely navigate you from point A to point B is not only stupid but also irresponsible; particularly if you are with others who are depending on you. In the wild there are plenty of "dead spots" and all electronics need to be charged, which is not always as easy as it sounds.

© Christopher Goldblatt

SOLAR PANEL AND BATTERY

Electronic gadgets all have one fatal flaw: they run on batteries and batteries die. You can prepare for this eventuality by keeping a solar charging panel or a panel with a battery inside

your EDC bag. Another common survival scenario is the survivor who was able to contact help but had limited ability to vector them in to their location because their cell phone died. Having the ability to recharge your devices could be the difference between a successful rescue and an unnecessary tragedy. Only carry electronic devices that can be recharged.

550 CORD

One of the most versatile items to have with you any time you head out on an excursion is mil-spec 550 parachute cord, a lightweight nylon kernmantle rope originally used in the suspension lines of parachutes. You can remove the inner seven lines from the outer shell of the cord and use them for additional cordage. With 550 belts, wristbands,

© Christopher Goldblatt

shoelaces, and all the other ways 550 cord is presented, there really is no excuse for not having at least a few yards on you in a time of need. You can purchase 550 cord that has trip wire and monofilament wire as well as a fire wick cord in addition to the other inner nylon cords. These make excellent additions to your survival posture, as they will give you options for fire starting, fishing, trapping, and many other applications.

Green Berets often use 550 cord to "dummy-cord" off their sensitive and high dollar items to their gear or to themselves so that they don't get lost in the heat of battle. After tying off the knot and cutting off the free running ends of the 550 cord it is customary to use a lighter to melt down the ends onto the knot in order to mitigate the chances of the knot coming loose.

© Christopher Goldblatt

100 MPH TAPE (DUCT TAPE)

One item you should never leave the house without is 100 MPH tape. It weighs next to nothing, it can be torn into thin strips and wrapped multiple times around other essential items such as lighters, water bottles or canteens, and many other items so that you always have some when you need some.

You can even put a few strips on the cover of this survival guide before you put it in your EDC bag. In a survival scenario you can use it as lashing material, to make repairs, and for thousands of other purposes. The fact is that 100 MPH tape is a military issue item but the civilian equivalent, duct tape, has a huge spectrum of products that range from  mediocre brands that don't work that great to brands such as Gorilla Tape® which work exceptionally well. The bottom line is that while any duct tape is better than no duct tape, in many cases you do get what you pay for with this product.

SURVIVAL PSYCHOLOGY

A large part of what drives a person to give up is often all in their head. When human beings are placed in situations that they either fear because they are new to them and feel ill-equipped or because the consequences of failure are catastrophic, they experience what is called the natural stress response. The more stress a person is under, the more likely they are to experience a number of physical, cognitive, and emotional reactions such as:

- Difficulty making decisions
- Angry outbursts
- Forgetfulness
- Low energy levels
- Constant worrying
- Propensity for mistakes
- Thoughts about death or suicide
- Trouble getting along with others
- Withdrawing from others
- Hiding from responsibilities
- Carelessness

If you find yourself thrown into a wilderness survival situation, do not panic. Take a moment to collect your thoughts and take a few slow, deep breaths. Your next decision could have life or death consequences and your brain will need all the oxygen it can get to think clearly and decisively. You cannot control the source of your stress but you can control your reaction to it! Stay calm, assess your situation and resources, make a plan, and execute it. Remember that you can always revise the plan as needed. If you are with others, do not allow stress to make you work against one another. Instead, work together as a team. Divide the labor of survival evenly and fairly based on each person's individual abilities.

THE EIGHT PILLARS OF WILDERNESS SURVIVAL

Many survival and emergency preparedness experts today use the pyramid approach to survival prioritization, putting food, water, shelter, and security in the largest block at the base of the pyramid and then community, sustainability, and higher needs in smaller brackets at the top of the pyramid. The basis for this eight-pillar system is that the survivor uses situational awareness to recognize which of the eight pillars of **food, water, shelter, security, communication, health and first aid, survival navigation, and firecraft** are most important at that moment. With this system, no one pillar takes priority over another. It is up to the survivor to assess their situation and then choose the pillar that is needed most to survive in the situation at hand. Much like a rifle pop-up target range where a shooter is expected to hit the closest and generally more dangerous targets first before engaging the targets that stand at the greatest distance, the survivor needs to prioritize the pillars and choose the pillar that is most urgent and necessary to save their life under the circumstances.

Survival is all about assessing the situation, coming up with a plan, and following through by implementing that plan. You must be flexible and understand that survival is a fluid and always changing situation, and when the survival environment changes you need to be ready to stop what you're doing and move to concentrate on the closest threat.

Failing to recognize this, not having good situational awareness, and becoming hyper-focused on a less pressing pillar can be the difference between life and death in a survival situation.

Food Procurement

The first pillar of emergency preparedness is food. The food pillar encompasses food procurement, storage, preparation, and sustainability. Food procurement can be further broken down into building traps and snares to catch game, survival techniques for fishing, and basic hunting skills for small game using field expedient weapons that you build on your own as well as manufactured weapons such as slingshots, air rifles, and small caliber firearms like the .22 caliber rifle.

Food procurement also includes a solid understanding of the edible plants in the area that you live in or are traveling to as well as understanding how to apply the universal edibility test by touching, tasting, then eating plants one part at a time with long intervals in between where you look for symptoms of food poisoning or an allergic or inflammatory reaction to the plant part in question.

Bushcraft food storage touches only some of the more basic methods of preserving food like smoking meats and salting.

UNIVERSAL EDIBILITY TEST

Warning: Eating poisonous plants can be harmful or deadly! The universal edibility test is used by Green Berets in emergency situations where they have had to use their expertise in wilderness survival to survive and return to friendly lines. It is a slow, methodical technique used to mitigate the risk of the survivor ingesting toxic levels of an unidentified or unconfirmed potential food source. This test is not easy; particularly in a survival situation where your body may be starving for nutrients and your first impulse is to eat whatever presents itself to you. Take the time to follow the steps so that you don't make the lethal mistake of eating a poisonous plant and dying a painful death that could have been avoided through discipline and patience.

Here is how you apply the universal edibility test (if there are more than one of you, allow one person to do this and not the entire party, as there will be no one left to look after the survival needs of the party if everyone is sick from eating the same toxic plant):

1. Wait eight hours without eating so that your stomach is empty.
2. Select a plant that grows in sufficient quantity in the local area. Separate the part of the plant that you wish to test: the root, stem, leaf, or flower. Certain parts of plants may be poisonous while other parts may be edible.
3. Rub a portion of the plant part you have selected on your inner forearm. Wait fifteen minutes and look for any swelling, rash, or irritation.
4. Boil the plant part in changes of water. The toxic properties of many plants are water soluble or destroyed by heat. Cooking and discarding two changes of water can lessen the amount of poisonous material or remove it completely. These boiling periods should last at least five minutes each.
5. Place 1 teaspoon of the prepared plant part in your mouth and chew for five minutes, but do not swallow. If unpleasant effects occur (burning, bitter, or nauseating taste), remove the plant from your mouth at once and discard it as a food source. If no unpleasant effects occur, swallow the plant material and wait eight hours.
6. If after 8 hours no unpleasant effects have occurred (nausea, cramps, diarrhea), eat two tablespoonsful and wait eight hours. If no unpleasant effects have occurred at the end of this eight-hour period, the plant part may be considered edible. **If any side effects occur, attempt to induce vomiting immediately and seek medical attention as soon as possible.**
7. Completely document and sketch the plant in a logbook to refer to for future use. This will aid in future procurement of this plant. If plant properties have changed, you will have to repeat the plant testing procedure.
8. Repeat this same procedure for each of the remainder of the plant parts.

In an emergency situation, eating small amounts of charcoal has been known to help soothe the stomach.

HUNTING

While hunting is more of a technical skill set left to those who hunt game as a form of sustenance as well as those who hunt for sport or to supplement their diet, from a bushcraft survival perspective many if not all of the techniques used for modern-day hunting can be modified to fit the survival sce-

nario. The bottom line is that in order to be successful at hunting you must use stealth and cunning and have a deep understanding of habits and behaviors of the animal that you are seeking. Many animals have far greater use of their senses than humans do, so becoming a proficient hunter is something that requires education and lots of practice both in stalking and/or setting up a perch and in learning to become proficient with your choice of weapon. By learning how to hunt, you will help keep wildlife populations at healthy levels, supplement your food stores, become comfortable being alone in the wilderness, and increase your overall chances of surviving a real-world survival scenario.

STALKING:

Stalking is a skill that requires stealth in movement, camouflage, and a keen understanding of the animals and environment around you. When stalking an animal, movement should be slow and methodical, and you should camouflage your body to match the environment around you. To remain

stealthful while walking, put your weight on the outside of your forward foot first, then slowly roll it down, testing the ground as you go. Any time you can get the high ground on an animal you are stalking you will gain advantage, as it will mask your smell, and many animals (including humans) do not naturally look up when they walk. Another technique to stay quiet is to use the heel of your forward foot first; whatever works for you. As you walk, try and use the noises in the environment around you to mask your movement. If an animal sees you, freeze and observe. The animal may only be curious and not see you as a threat. Use extreme caution when hunting apex predators such as some species of bear or even large hooved animals like wild boar or moose, as if not mortally wounded they could easily come after you. It's is possible to go from hunter to hunted in seconds or to be charged and pummeled or eviscerated by an enraged beast.

Standoff: Putting an object like a tree, rock, or any feature of the terrain in between yourself and whatever you are stalking will help mask your signature and lower the odds that your prey will see you. A good way to remember this is that if you can't see it, it most likely cannot see you either. You can use standoff to close big distances between yourself and your prey, thereby increasing your odds of dispatching the animal in the quickest and most humane way.

> When hunting, try to keep the wind in your face in relation to the position of the animal you are stalking. In the natural world, most wild animals have incredibly advanced perception of their senses and can smell even the most subtle of odors, so keeping the wind in your face minimizes the chances of your being given away by your smell.

Perching: One of the most successful ways to hunt some animals is by taking up a stationary and stable position either up in a tree, in the high ground aiming down, or in a blind or hide on the ground but upwind from your prospective prey.

TRACKING

Whether you are hunting or trapping an animal, you first need to know where to find them. Learning how to track animals will not only help you find food, but can also lead you to water and/or potential shelter locations.

© Survivapedia

Trails and runs: Trails and runs are simply paths cut through the forest by animals trampling down foliage. Trails typically lead to watering holes, bedding down areas, and other locations that make up animal habitats.

Dens, burrows, and bedding down areas: These are areas where animals either sleep or seek refuge and safety from other predators and the weather.

Rubs: Male animals such as deer will often use their antlers to rub the bark off of young saplings and in many cases rub their scent or urinate on them in order to mark their territory.

Scratches: These are exactly what they sound like: scratches left by an animal on the ground or on trees.

Transference: Transference is when dirt or other natural materials like leaves, sticks, and rocks are moved from their original location to another due to the movement of an animal.

Compression: Compression is when dirt, sticks, or weeds are pressed down into the ground due to the weight of an animal that walked over the area.

Disturbance: A disturbance is when the natural order of a particular area has been disturbed. An example would be when leaves with dew on the forest floor have been shaken due to an animal traveling through, making the leaves appear different from the surrounding area.

Gait: The natural way that an animal walks is its gait.

Gallopers: Rodents are usually gallopers. When this type of animal moves forward, it pushes off with its back legs and propels its body forward, landing with its front feet side by side.

Diagonal walkers: Diagonal walkers move opposite sides of their bodies at the same time. Predatory animals are typically considered diagonal walkers.

Bounders: Animals with short legs and long bodies are considered bounders. Bounders walk by moving their front feet first, then bringing their back feet up behind them.

Pacers: Wide-bodied animals are usually pacers. Pacers tend to move both limbs on one side of their body at the same time.

Gnawing: Animals often chew or "gnaw" on twigs, bark, and other vegetation, leaving visual bite marks.

Scat: Scat is the solid waste or feces left by an animal. You can tell a lot about an animal's health, what it is eating, and how long since it was there by looking at its scat.

Spoor: Any time the actual track or footprint of an animal is visible, it is considered the animal's "spoor."

Reading spoor: Being able to identify the animal type, direction, and time since last at that location would be considered reading spoor.

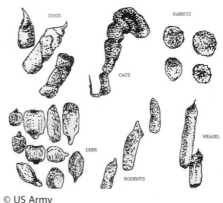

© US Army

TRAPPING

In a wilderness survival scenario, trapping may be your best bet when it comes to getting the proteins you will need to stay healthy and survive your ordeal. Instead of thinking big like trapping a wild boar, consider smaller game like rodents, lizards, and birds, as they tend to be easier to find and catch and they pose less risk of doing you harm. When it comes to trapping, it really is a numbers game. The more traps you can put out, the better chance you will have of catching anything. Remember to place the traps in line with known game trails and to camouflage them well. Traps come in many shapes and sizes, from deadfall traps that drop a crushing blow to their prey to snares that kill an animal by a noose that chokes it to death. Live traps such as nets, cages, and pits are intended to trap the animal in place but do not necessarily kill the animal. There are also clamping traps that use spring tension to trap an animal's appendages by biting down with powerful teeth that hold the animal in place. No matter what type of trap you are using, unless it is self-triggering, it will require a trigger to activate it. The two trigger types talked about in this book are the deadfall trigger and the snare trigger, and these two trigger systems can be applied to the majority of traps you will find ourself using in a wilderness survival scenario.

The eight general tips for trapping are:

1. Know the game you are trapping.
2. KISS (Keep It Simple, Stupid).
3. Set up traps in line with known animal activity.
4. Cover up your scent.
5. Use the right type of trap for the animal you are trapping.
6. Use the right sized trap for the animal you are trapping.
7. Check traps often.
8. Bait your traps.

TYPES OF DEADFALL TRIGGERS

THE SIMPLE TRIGGER

The simple trigger is one of the easiest trigger systems that you can construct, and it takes the least moving parts to make.

What you will need:
Post stick: This stick should be straight, about 10"–12" long and ½" in diameter.

© Brian Morris

Bait stick: The bait stick needs to be straight, about 6"–8" long and ¼" in diameter.

Bait: You will need the appropriate bait for the game you are attempting to catch.

To construct a simple trigger, follow these steps:

Step 1: Bore a hole about ¼" in diameter through the center of the post stick.

Step 2: Carefully cut to the left and right of the hole so that the post stick splits in half into two shorter pieces. **Tip:** Peel off a strip of bark where the two base sticks join so that you know exactly how to join them back together again.

Step 3: Sharpen the tip of one end of the bait stick and whittle down the other end so that it fits snugly into the hole of the other base stick.

Step 4: Add bait to bait stick.

Step 5: Holding the two base sticks together at the exact spot they were cut, insert the bait stick firmly into the hole of the base stick. You should be able to hold the entire trigger in one hand.

Step 6: Holding the trigger system in one hand, lift the deadfall with the other and allow its weight to rest on top of the base stick with the stick standing at about a 45° angle. The weight and balance of the deadfall should be able to rest on the trigger system independently.

THE FIGURE 4 TRIGGER

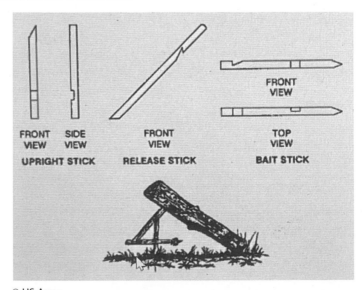

© US Army

The figure 4 trigger can be used to set a cage to fall, trapping prey, or to set a large, flat rock, log, or other heavy object to fall and crush prey. The advantages of a figure 4 are that malfunction is less likely because there are fewer parts to fail and that a well-constructed figure 4 can be quickly set with one hand, leaving the other hand free to lift the deadfall up and set the trigger in place. The disadvantages are that this trigger design requires some level of skill to cut out the precise angles needed to get the trigger set and hold in place and it is not the most sensitive method of trigger design to set off.

What you will need:
Post stick (upright stick): This stick should be straight, about 8"–10" long, ½" in diameter, and "Y" off at the top.
Bait stick: The bait stick needs to be straight, a bit wider than the diameter of the hole, and about 6"–10" long. **Tip:** Even in a perfect scenario where all three of your sticks are the exact same size, this trigger design requires close tolerances and precise angles in order to have a trigger that sets and holds well. To create a figure 4 trigger system without the need for a mathematical equation, your best bet is to start off finding one stick that is between 1½'–2' long and as straight as you can find. You will want this stick to be around 1" in diameter. Use the stick to get your three sticks to construct this trigger.
Bait: You will need the appropriate bait for the game you are attempting to catch.
Lever stick (release stick): This stick should be straight, about 10"–12" long, and ½" in diameter.
Deadfall or cage: Deadfalls should be flat on the side that will hit the ground and weigh about five times or more the weight of the animal you are trying to dispatch. If you are going for a live catch with a cage, remember to weight the cage enough so that your catch will not be able to lift it and escape.

To construct a figure 4 trigger, follow these steps:
Step 1: Starting with the post stick, carve a flat notch about an inch long and ¼"–½" wide about a quarter of the way up from the base of the stick. Shave the top of the post stick to a flat edge.
Step 2: The bait stick must have an almost identical carving as the post stick but located ⅓ of the way down from the top of the stick; the idea being that it will marry up with the post stick like a Lincoln log. Now, sharpen the tip closest to the post stake notch to a point (for skewering your bait). Finally, at the base end of the bait stick, about 2" from the end, cut a "V" notch for the lever stick to lock into.

Step 3: On the lever stick, carve a "V" notch ¼"–½" in depth about ¼ of the way up from the end of it. Shave the opposite end of the lever stick to a flat edge.

Step 4: Stand up the post stick. Take the bait stick (baited) and match it up horizontally with the identical notch on the post stick. Now, place the flat-edged end of the lever stick into the "V" notch of the bait stick and the flat-edged end of the base stick into the "V" notch of the lever stick. When done correctly, you should be able to hold the entire trigger together with one hand.

Step 5: Hold the trigger in one hand and, with the opposite hand, lift up the front edge of the object you are using as a deadfall and gently rest it on the tip of the lever stick. It should only be necessary to raise the object to about two to three times the height of the animal you are attempting to dispatch. If done correctly, the weight of the object will be enough to hold the notched wood in place.

THE PAIUTE TRIGGER

The Paiute trigger and the figure 4 trigger are similar. The major difference between the two is that, instead of another wooden stick, the Paiute trigger relies on a length of taut cordage and toggle to hold the trigger together along with the weight of the deadfall itself and the pressure applied to the toggle by the bait stick. While both the

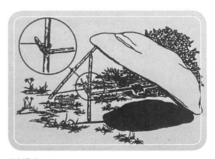

© US Army

Paiute and figure 4 require some level of skill to construct and set in place, the Paiute trigger has the advantage of being the more sensitive of the two to set off. Both triggers can be used to set a cage to fall trapping prey or to set a large, flat rock to crush prey. **Note:** This example is to catch a small rat or field mouse–sized animal. The stick dimensions and cordage strength will need to increase if you plan to scale up the trigger to hold a great deal of weight. Be aware that the heavier the weight, the more difficult one person may find setting the trigger.

What you will need:

Cordage: You will want at least 12" of cordage so that you have enough to make final size adjustments.

Lever stick: This stick should be straight, about 10"–12" long, and ½" in diameter.

Toggle stick: This stick only needs to be about 2" long, ¼" in diameter, and it will help if you can cut it down to a flat rectangle shape about ¼" thick.

Bait stick: The bait stick needs to be straight, about the same diameter as the toggle stick, and about 12"–14" long. **Tip:** Find the crack or crevice at the base of your deadfall, then use it to make the final adjustments on how long your bait stick needs to be.

Bait: You will need the appropriate bait for the game you are attempting to catch.

Post stick: This stick should be straight, about 8"–10" long, about ½" in diameter, and "Y" off at the top.

Deadfall or cage: Deadfalls should be flat on the side that will hit the ground and weigh about five times or more the weight of the animal you are trying to dispatch. If you are going for a live catch with a cage, remember to weight the cage enough so that your catch will not be able to lift it and escape. While a log will work as a deadfall, a flat rock will be far more efficient because it offers a kill area that covers a great deal more surface area. If you must use a log, place multiple wooden stakes on either side of the log so that when the trigger is activated the log will fall straight down and not roll left or right.

To construct a Paiute trigger, follow these steps:

Step 1: Tie one end of your cordage to the end of the lever stick. Use overhand knots at first until you determine the exact length of cordage needed to set the trap. At that point you can secure with a square knot.

Step 2: Leaving about 8"–10" of cordage in between, tie the other end of the cordage to the center of the toggle stick.

Step 3: Sharpen the bait stick and skewer your bait to the end of the stick at the tip. You can also rub bait onto the end of the bait stick if you prefer.

Step 4: Stand up the post stick by the edge of the deadfall with the "Y" end up. Insert the stringless end of the lever stick into the "Y" of the post stick with about 1"–2" of lever stick coming out the other end facing the deadfall.

Step 5: Lift the front end of the deadfall and let it rest on about an inch or so of the protruding end of the lever stick. You will know you are doing it correctly if you can rest the total weight of the deadfall by applying downward pressure on the end of the lever stick with the string tied to it.

Step 6: Wrap the toggle stick halfway around the post stick. If you are doing it correctly, at this point you should be able to hold up the entire deadfall simply by holding the toggle stick in place.

Step 7: The final step is to lock the toggle stick in place with the bait stick by placing the blunt end of the bait stick onto the flat surface of the toggle stick and securing the baited end of the bait stick into a predetermined crack or crevice on the base of the deadfall.

> Trapping is a numbers game. The more traps you set, the more chances you will have of catching prey. Create a trap line by setting in place a series of traps and marking them in such a way that you can easily identify their location but potential prey will not be tipped off and avoid it. You can use burned wood to draw signs on nearby trees or even draw a map showing all your traps.

SNARING

Snaring is an effective way to take game. Snaring relies on a cord or line connected to a noose that uses spring tension such as that provided by a bent sapling to activate the noose and kill the prey. Snares normally rely on a trigger system to release the spring tension and activate the noose with the exception of self-activating snares such as squirrel poles that are set off by the prey's own body weight and momentum as they put their head through the noose and fall off the pole.

Three things to consider when emplacing a snare:
- Location
- Presentation
- Construction

Noose Sizes and Ground Clearance for Snaring (by Animal)

Animal	Noose Size	Ground Clearance
Squirrel	2½–3 inches	½–1½ inches
Rabbit	4–5½ inches	1½–3 inches
Raccoon	6 inches	3–4 inches
Fox	7–10 inches	8–10 inches
Coyote	12–14 inches	12 inches
Bobcat	9 inches	8 inches

HOW TO CONSTRUCT A SNARE TOGGLE TRIGGER

Step 1: Cut an inverted or upside down "V" into the trigger tree. Carve down a ¼"–½" diameter stick into a 2"–3"-long toggle that will fit into the inverted "V" notch on the trigger tree and hold in place when upward pressure is applied.

Step 2: Tie one end of a 1'–2' line to one end of the toggle and the other end of the line to the spring tree on the opposite side of the trap.

Step 3: Tie a non-slip knot such as a bowline knot to one end of the wire. Next, loop the free-running end of the wire through the non-slip loop and cinch it down to a noose the appropriate diameter for the game you are attempting to catch. Now, take the free-running end of the noose and tie or connect it to the toggle.

Step 4: Pull down on the tip of the spring tree and place the toggle into the inverted "V" notch until the spring tension from the sapling is holding the toggle in place.

Step 5: Carefully position the noose into place so that it is open and in the best position for the prey to get caught up in the noose if it trips the snare. You can push small "Y"-shaped twigs into the ground to hold open the noose. You can also put bait by the noose of the snare trap to attract animals to the trap.

SPRING TENSION TRIGGER

To set a snare you can use any trigger system you like or it can be "self-triggered," meaning the snare is tied off and the animal's weight and momentum are what cause the snare to tighten and kill the prey. Here is a simple example of how to set a sapling toggle triggered snare:

© US Army

Step 1: Find a place that has two saplings 2"–4" apart growing on opposite sides of the game trail that you'd like to channel your prey into. **Tip:** To increase your odds of catching something, find a location where you've seen your desired prey or signs of foot traffic such as tracks and game trails.

Step 2: Cut an inverted "V" notch toward the base of the first sapling and angle the notch slightly upward in the cut.

Step 3: Use 2 "Y"-shaped twigs to keep the loop in your line open to the desired circumference height and width (see chart above on page 44).

Step 4: Construct a toggle out of a small piece of wood about 2"–3" long. Tie a small piece of line to either end of the toggle.

Step 5: Tie a line that is about 2'–3' long to the center of the loop on the toggle.

Step 6: Tie the free-running end of the toggle line to the tip of a strong sapling.

Step 7: Pulling down on the sapling, set the spring tension line by setting the toggle in place inside of the notch on the bottom of the anchor tree. **Note:** It may take some adjustments to get the toggle to remain set by the upward pressure created by the spring tension of the toggle line.

Step 8: Gently tie the free-running end of the noose to the loop of the toggle line. The idea is that the animal will walk through the noose and activate the trigger by pulling the toggle out of the notch in the anchor tree and setting off the sapling which will snap back and pull the noose tight onto the animal and suspend them from the sapling. **Note:** It is very important to ensure that the toggle line is short enough to suspend the animal in the air and not give it a chance to escape. A good rule of thumb is that the line should be about half the length of the height of the sapling.

SELF-ACTIVATED TRIGGER TRAPS
Squirrel pole:

Step 1: Locate a tree that is frequently seen having squirrels run up and down its trunk.

Step 2: Find a stick that is about 3' long and 1"–2" in diameter.

Step 3: Using wire from your survival kit, tie off a series of snares around the circumference of the stick spiraling down from the top to the bottom.

Step 4: Lean the stick at about a 45° angle against the tree. As squirrels climb up and down the tree, they will soon use the stick to climb onto and off the tree, getting their heads caught up in the snare. Eventually, they will fall off the stick and be strangled to death. It is not uncommon to have multiple kills hanging on a squirrel pole when you check your traps.

© Brian Morris

Reptiles and Amphibians

If you get the opportunity to catch one of these animals for food, you will find that they are pleasant to the taste and provide a ton of much needed protein. Use extreme caution, as there is no antivenom in the bush and some of these animals can deliver a painful bite that can lead to serious infection or worse. Use a flashlight to stun a frog, then bash it with a blunt object. When killing a snake, pin it down at the neck just below the head, then use a sharp knife to remove the head and three inches or more of the neck. Treat the head with caution, as a snake can deliver a bite even after its head is removed from its body. Snapping turtles can be handled by the tail. Use caution, as they can take off a finger with their powerful bite. Keep the head facing away from you. All meat on the turtle is edible once thoroughly cooked but the neck meat is most prized for its flavor.

© Brian Morris   © Survivapedia

KILLING TRAPPED ANIMALS FOR FOOD

If you trap or catch an animal and it is still alive, you want to dispatch it in the easiest, most humane, and fastest method available. The best way to quickly kill an animal is with a firearm. If one is not available to you, you can strike the animal behind the head with a blunt object to render it unconscious and then either cut its throat from ear to ear or spear/stab through the armpit area directly into the heart, using your blade to "scramble" the heart by making a circular rotation with your blade, then pumping the animal's chest with your knee or hand to help it bleed out. Larger animals can be hung from a tree by their hind legs to allow it to bleed out and be processed. Use caution not to puncture the organs such as the gallbladder, intestines, or bladder, as the fluids inside the organs can easily taint the meat.

It is not only humane to dispatch an animal as quickly as possible, but it will also have a major effect on the taste of the meat in many cases. Animals

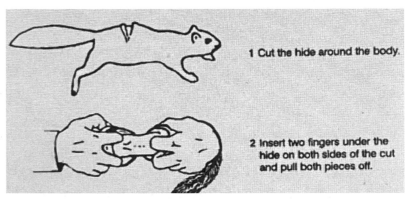

1 Cut the hide around the body.

2 Insert two fingers under the hide on both sides of the cut and pull both pieces off.

© US Army

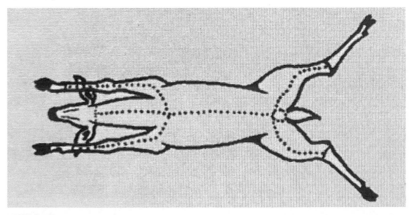

© US Army

who suffer great stress prior to death are often tougher in texture and have a less appetizing taste due to the amount of stress enzymes released compared to animals that are killed swiftly.

Preparing Animals to Cook and Eat

To process small game, make an incision through the fur across its back, then pull the coat off the animal by pulling your hands apart. Degut and cook thoroughly. Larger animals should be hung to process if possible. Make an incision from neck to anus and degut. Snakes and reptiles can be prepared similarly. To prepare fish, descale them and make an incision along the belly to degut them.

FISHING

Depending upon your location, resources available to you, type of water source, and type and/or size of fish, certain fishing equipment may be needed.

Expedient hooks: It is always a good idea to carry fishhooks of varied sizes in your survival kit but if you don't have any they are easy to construct. Below are a few examples:

Fishing spear: If you are near shallow water (about waist deep) where fish are large and plentiful, you can spear them.

© Brian Morris

You can purchase a premanufactured fishing spearhead to be kept in your EDC bag or you can simply construct your own. To construct a fishing spear, simply split the tip of a straight sapling stick that is about 5'–7' in length. Place a small rock in between the three-way split and lash it at the base. Last, sharpen each of the three tips into a barb. To spear fish, place the spear point into the water and slowly move it toward the fish. Then, with a quick trust, quickly impale the fish to the water bottom. Hold the spear with one hand and grab the fish with your free hand.

© Brian Morris

© Brian Morris

FISH TRAPS

A fish trap can be either something you construct or a way of using a fish's natural habitat and simply blocking off any way for it to escape. You may trap fish using several methods. Fish baskets are one method. You construct them by lashing several sticks together with vines into a funnel shape and closing the top, leaving a hole large enough for the fish to swim through. You can also use traps to catch saltwater fish, as schools regularly approach the shore with the incoming tide and often move parallel to the shore. Pick a location at

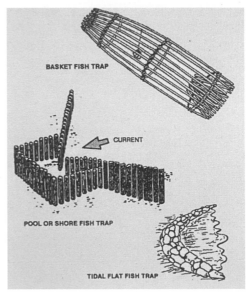

BASKET FISH TRAP

CURRENT

POOL OR SHORE FISH TRAP

TIDAL FLAT FISH TRAP

© Survivapedia

high tide and build the trap at low tide. On rocky shores, use natural rock pools. On coral islands, use natural pools on the surface of reefs by blocking the openings as the tide recedes. On sandy shores, use sandbars and the ditches they enclose. Build the trap as a low stone wall extending outward into the water, forming an angle with the shore.

FISHING SET LINES/TROTLINE

Setting a fishing set line is a great way to multitask, as you can leave it alone to fish for you while you attend to other survival tasks. Be sure to make several of them to increase your chances of catching food. To make a trot line, simply run a horizontal line across a body of water and either anchor

it into the ground on the opposite sides of the shoreline of small creeks and rivers or use sticks to anchor into the water bottom and run your trotline between the two sticks. Make sure to tie strands of fishing line or thin cordage to the trotline with a hook attached to the free-running end and space the lines far enough apart so that they will not become tangled in the water.

Bait

No matter what you are fishing for you will most likely need to use bait. The best bait is using what fish already eat naturally. It may take some time experimenting with what you can find in the area to find out what the fish are biting at on any given day. Fishing takes patience.

© Survivapedia

NETTING

You can make a net out of any cordage but it's much easier with a thin nylon line such as the inner cordage of paracord. Use rocks tied to the bottom of the net to keep it on the water's bottom. Start with a single horizontal line and tie multiple lines, dropping vertically and spacing them an inch or less apart. Next, tie cordage in a crisscross pattern horizontal with the same spacing as your vertical lines. Once you have your net constructed, tie each end of it off to a tall stick that you can push into the water's bottom to hold the net in place. If there is a strong current, you can tie rocks to the bottom of the net to keep the net open and maximize your chances of catching any fish.

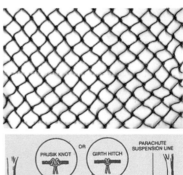

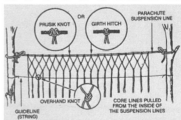

© Survivapedia

FISH POISON

Another way to catch fish is by using poison. Poison works quickly. It allows you to remain concealed while it takes effect. It also enables you to catch several fish at one time. When using fish poison, be sure to gather all of the affected fish because many dead fish floating downstream could alert other fish and keep them away. Some plants that grow in warm regions of the world contain rotenone, a substance that stuns or kills cold-blooded animals but does not harm persons who eat the animals. The best place to use rotenone, or rotenone-producing plants, is in ponds or the headwaters of small streams containing fish. Rotenone works quickly on fish in water 70°F (21°C) or above. The fish rise helplessly to the surface. It works slowly in water 50°F–70°F (10°C–21°C) and is ineffective in water below 50°F (10°C).

The following plants and substances, used as indicated, will stun or kill fish:

Tephrosia:
This species of small shrubs bears beanlike pods, grows throughout the tropics, and contains rotenone. Crush or bruise bundles of leaves and stems and throw them into the water.

Lime:
You can get lime from commercial sources and in agricultural areas that use large quantities of it. You may produce your own by burning coral or seashells. Throw the lime into the water and wait for the fish to float to the surface as the lime removes the oxygen from the water.

Nut husks:
Crush green husks from butternuts or black walnuts. Throw the husks into the water and wait for the stunned fish to float to the surface.

FORAGING AND GATHERING

The greatest food procurement technique in a wilderness survival scenario is the one that is most abundant, requires the least amount of energy to acquire, provides the greatest amount of nutrients and protein pound-for-pound to the survivor, and poses the least physical risk to procure. Mollusks,

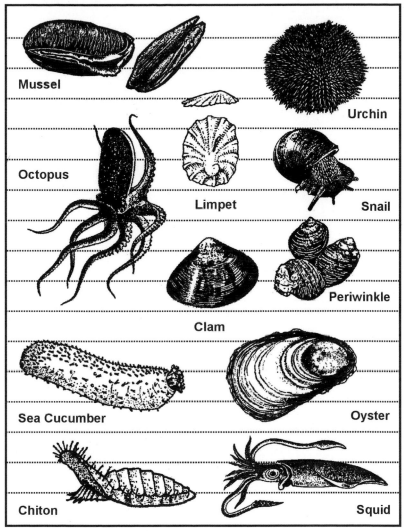

Mussel

Urchin

Octopus

Limpet

Snail

Periwinkle

Clam

Sea Cucumber

Oyster

Chiton

Squid

© US Army

small lizards, (some) snakes, insects, arachnids, and plant life all fall into these criteria and should be your priority when deciding what type of food to search for.

INSECTS AND ARACHNIDS
The inverted v trap:
The easiest way to trap small insects is the inverted v trap. The inverted trap works great for insects as well as small lizards, frogs, rodents, and other small animals.

Making this trap is as easy as 1, 2, 3:

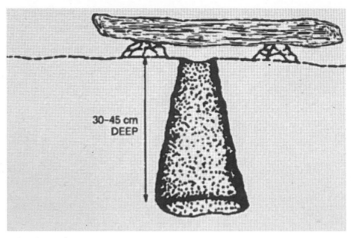

© Survivapedia

1. Start by digging a hole about an inch deep.
2. The hole of the trap should be dug in the form of an inverted v with the top of the hole being far smaller than the diameter of the hole's base.
3. Once the hole is dug, find four small rocks about 2"–3" tall and put them in four corners around the outside of the hole and far enough apart to support and suspend a large, flat rock above the hole. As animals move under the rock to seek shade or hide from predators, they will fall into the hole and be unable to get out due to the inverted slope angle of the hole.

Why insects and arachnids make great survival food:
Insects and arachnids are the most abundant life-forms on earth and are an excellent survival food. They are easy to catch and provide 65%–80% protein, compared to 20% for beef. They aren't too appetizing, but personal bias has no place in a survival situation. The focus must remain on maintaining your health.

Pound for pound when it comes to both time and energy as well as nutritional value, insects and arachnids are one of the best survival foods out there. Catching these animals is relatively simple. Most times all you need to do is roll over a large rock to find a survival meal's worth of little critters! To learn about how to prepare these animals to eat, refer to Chapter 10 on page 173.

Edible insects and arachnids:

- Insect larvae

- Grasshoppers

- Beetles

- Ants

- Termites

- Worms

© Brian Morris

Foraging for insects:
One must be careful not to expend more energy harvesting food than can be replaced. For example, catching insects such as grasshoppers can become exasperating and tiring whereas a grub can be plucked from a rotting tree with little to no energy expenditure.

Foraging for vegetation:
There are few places without some type of edible vegetation. Plants contain protein, fiber, vitamins, minerals, and carbohydrates. While some plants can be harmful or even fatal if ingested, the benefits outweigh the risks, so if you are in an area with vegetation in a survival situation you should put the plant(s) to the universal edibility test. The more plants you can positively identify, the less time and risk you will have to take to see if a plant is safe to eat.

Plants to Avoid

- All mushrooms (unless you are an expert). Mushrooms add little to no nutritional value and are often dangerous to a point where the risk outweighs the reward.
- Any plant that presents milky sap.
- Yellow and white berries are almost always poisonous.
- Any plant with shiny leaves is normally poisonous.
- Plants that are irritants to the skin should not be eaten.
- Avoid pea- and bean-like vegetation unless you can make a positive identification that it is edible.

The following seven plants are common to most temperate environments on earth and are all safe for consumption:

- Wild onions: all parts

- Cattail: root, stalk, and stem

- Bull thistle: flowers

- Juniper tree:

- All conifers: cambium layer, needles, and nuts within the cones

- Dandelion: all parts, cooked or raw

Preparing an edible plant to eat:

Survival is 90 percent keeping yourself healthy and uninjured. Because of this, you don't want to take uncalculated risks, particularly when it comes to food. Even if you can recognize a plant as edible, you should still boil it to remove any bacteria or harmful residues the plant may con-

tain. Boiling will have the added benefit of removing bitterness which will make the plant more palatable and easier to eat.

Foods with Extended Shelf life

There are many foods on the market with shelf lives of ten and up to twenty-five years under proper storage conditions. Keeping several days' worth of extended shelf life meals in your EDC bag is a smart move and will give you some breathing room if you ever find yourself in a survival situation.

© Brian Morris

Water Procurement

The third pillar of survival is water, including water procurement, water preparation, and water storage. More than three-quarters of the human body is composed of liquids, so water is arguably one of the most important resources in a survival situation. Stress, exertion, and/ or exposure to heat or cold can cause a loss or outflow of body fluids that must be replaced quickly if you are going to be able to function effectively in a survival situation. Exactly how much water a person needs to survive and function in any given situation varies greatly. A good rule of thumb is one gallon per person per day, but this is dependent on the factors of activity, environment, and level of perspiration. In a harsh environment like the desert, the body loses fluids at an alarming rate through perspiration, respiration, and urination. In cold temperatures, a person needs as much as two liters of water a day to maintain efficient thermoregulation. It is up to you in a survival situation to ensure that you locate, treat, drink, and store enough water to survive the situation that you are in.

In the end, what matters most is that you find a way to restore the amount of water and electrolytes equal to those that you lost in the specific survival situation that you are in. If you start out dehydrated, you will be playing catch-up. Hydrate your body first and then fill canteens, but the first thing you will have to do is locate a water source. While one of the most effective ways to treat water is to boil it, there are many other ways to treat water. Once you have located and treated your water, you will need to find a way to store it. There are multiple methods of doing this, as you will discover in this chapter. Always remember that without water in a survival situation you will most assuredly die, so take this pillar seriously and survive to live another day.

Bird flight in the early morning or late afternoon might indicate the direction to water.

What to look for when determining your water intake needsı
Thirst is not a strong enough sensation to determine how much water your body needs to survive. The best thing you can do is drink plenty of water any time it is available. Dehydration is a major threat to the ability of your body to function properly.

- A loss of only 5 percent of your body fluids causes thirstiness, irritability, queasiness, and loss in strength.
- A 10 percent loss can cause headache, vertigo, inability to walk, and a tingling sensation in the arms and legs.
- A 15 percent loss can cause blurred vision, pain when urinating, a swollen tongue, loss of hearing, and a feeling of numbness in the skin.
- A loss of more than 15 percent body fluids could result in death.

The three most important aspects of this precious commodity are how to find it, how to treat it, and how to store it so that you always have access to this priceless liquid of life when you need it.

Tip: Pale yellow urine indicates adequate hydration.

FINDING WATER

LAKES, RIVERS, AND STREAMS
Water from a lake, stream, river, or other natural fresh water source can be processed for consumption. Remember that just because it's a natural water source does not mean that it is ready to drink as is. You must first disinfect all water in order to render it potable and safe to drink.

NATURAL SPRINGS
Springs are formed because of the water in an aquifer overflowing onto the land's surface. The water that springs produce is most often pure and ready

to drink but you can never be sure so it is always a smart idea to purify spring water prior to consumption if the water quality is unknown.

OCEAN/SEA (SALT WATER)

Do not drink salt water without desalination or distillation. Boiling will not remove the salt from water. It concentrates it. The water vapor or steam that is produced when salt water is boiled is free of salt water, so the condensation produced from boiled salt water can be used to drink.

> **Warning:** Drinking salt water will lead to a slow and agonizing death.

RAINWATER

Rainwater is safe to drink as is in most cases but water collection devices can often be contaminated so if you are not confident that yours is free of contaminants, you should consider purifying your rainwater again before you drink it.

DEW/CONDENSATION

There are many ways to collect dew by way of bushes, plants, and trees. Dew is a pure and safe form of drinking water once collected. A good way to procure dew for drinking is to let it absorb into a clean cloth and then ring out the cloth into a container or into your mouth. A

military and fieldcraft trick is to tie cotton bandanas or towels to your shins and walk through grass that is covered with dew.

SNOW AND ICE

Snow and ice make an excellent source of water as long as they are melted before consumption. If you are not certain that the snow or ice is pure, be sure to purify it prior to consumption. **Warning:** Eating snow or ice to stay hydrated in a survival situation where you are out in the elements is a bad idea because this can cause you to suffer from hypothermia, which can be deadly.

VEGETATION

Even in the most arid environments, water can be found in vegetation if you know where to look for it. Root, pulp, leaves, and stems all contain water. **Note:** If you are not certain that the species of vegetation you are trying to extract water from is not poisonous, it is imperative to either leave it be or, at a minimum, purify the water and do the universal edibility test prior to consumption.

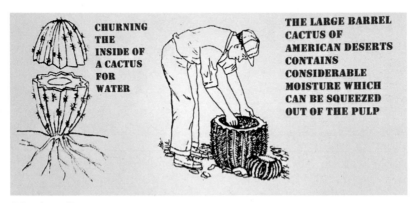

CHURNING THE INSIDE OF A CACTUS FOR WATER

THE LARGE BARREL CACTUS OF AMERICAN DESERTS CONTAINS CONSIDERABLE MOISTURE WHICH CAN BE SQUEEZED OUT OF THE PULP

© Survivapedia

GROUND WATER

In brackish or freshwater estuaries, where there are often small patches of dry land adjacent to swamps and wetlands, you can dig a hole in the ground next to that body of water and drink the water that seeps through the soil into the hole. That said, you should still try to purify the water again if you have the ability to do so.

ANIMAL LIFE

While life is not always an absolute indicator that water is available in the area; it can certainly help you in procuring this essential lifesaving liquid when you need it the most. Observing wildlife is a great way to obtain the location of water. You can also get water directly from 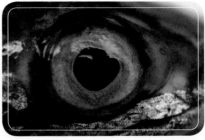 certain animals. An example of this is extracting fresh water from fish by eating their eyeballs. The eyeballs of fish contain a fluid that is mainly pure unsalted water and is safe to drink. To get the eyeball out, you can squeeze the fish and suck the eyeball out, using your teeth to sever the back of the eyeball, or use a spoon to cut the eyeball out. You can also drink the aqueous fluid along the fish's spine, as this is mainly composed of fresh water. To get it, carefully cut the spine in half and drink the fluid inside. There's no guarantee that this source will keep you alive, but it beats the hell out of drinking nothing or, even worse, drinking salt water, as that will only lead to a painful and delirious death. You can even extract some pure water from a fish's flesh. Once you have a small pile of diced flesh, place it in a piece of cotton cloth, then wring the cloth into a cup or your mouth to catch the lymphatic fluids that flow out, which are mostly water. The Latin root of lymph means "clear water."

VINES

Look for vines running up tall trees. Pry a vine away from its tree and, using a sharp knife or machete, sever the vine and drink or collect the clear water that flows from the vine. The larger in diameter the vine is, the more water it can hold. Not all vines will produce vast amounts of water, but in a survival scenario you want to drink every drop of water you can get.

- Cut bark (*do not* drink milky sap).
- If juice is clear and water-like, cut as large a piece of vine as possible (cut the top first).
- Pour into hand to check the smell, color, and taste to determine if drinkable.
- *Do not* touch vine to lips.
- When water flow stops, cut off six inches of the opposite end and water should flow again.

Caution: When searching for water in vines, make sure that you are drinking clear, liquid water, as some vines will produce a white, sappy liquid that is highly bitter to the tase and can cause extreme stomach distress if consumed.

ABOVEGROUND SOLAR STILL

The concept behind an aboveground still is condensation. To construct an aboveground still you will need access to (nonpoisonous) vegetation such as green leaves from a bush, plant, or tree, a clear plastic bag (a 1-gallon resealable bag is perfect), a small rock or weighted object, some light cordage, and if you can find one, a straw, hollow reed, or piece of tubing. Fill the vegetation in the plastic bag about ½ to ¾ full. Place a small rock or weighted object in the bag and find something to clog the drinking end of your straw, hollow reed, or piece of tubing with or bend it over on itself and secure it so it will not leak, then put it into the opening of the bag. Fill the bag with air and tie it shut with the light cordage and the straw, hollow reed, or piece of tubing protruding out of the end. A straw will allow you to get water from the bag without opening it up but if you aren't able to find one you can just open the bag each time you are ready to empty out any water that has accumulated. To produce water, take the tied bag and place it on a slope with a small rock or weighted object positioned at the low point of the bag's orientation. Make sure the slope is located in an area where it will be exposed to optimal sunlight. Allow time for the heat of the sun to cause condensation inside of the bag. As water collects, you can harvest the water by drinking it through the straw. It is highly recommended that if you plan to use a still you make several of them in order to ensure that you produce enough water to survive.

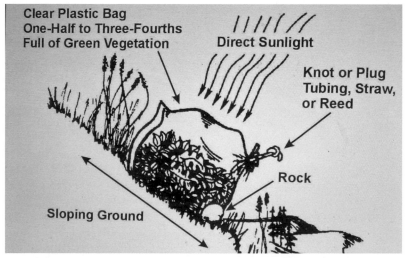

© Survivapedia

BELOWGROUND SOLAR STILL

The concept behind a belowground still is similar to that of an aboveground still but it is constructed differently. To construct a belowground still you will need something to dig a hole with, a container to hold water in, a clear plastic sheet, and a small rock or weight. Start by digging a hole about a meter in diameter and a foot deep. Place the drinking container in the center of the hole with the open end facing up to catch water. Put several handfuls of vegetation around the container to help speed up the condensation process. Stretch the plastic sheet over the top of the hole, then weight down the edges of the plastic sheet with dirt, rocks, or sand all around the outside edges of the hole. Take your small rock or weight and place it on top of the plastic sheet in the center just over the area where the container is located. If you have a straw or some tubing, you can plug it and place the open end into the water container. You can always just drink from the container itself if you don't have a straw. Make sure you construct your still in an area where it will receive maximum sunlight. You should try to find a spot where you believe the soil contains moisture such as a dry streambed. Allow the water to collect in the container so that you can drink water when you need it.

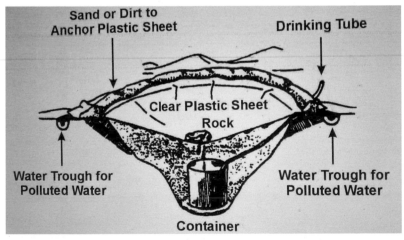

© Survivapedia

Caution: Always use nonpoisonous vegetation to augment the condensation process as poisonous vegetation may contaminate your water supply.

RAIN CATCH

You can easily construct a rain catch to channel water into a large container to be stored for a later date. Use a clean poncho, tarp, or shelter roof constructed with nonpoisonous leaf, bamboo, or wooden/rock shingles to create a surface to catch water and channel to a catch basin. Remember that once the rain touches your roof it is no longer "pure" and should be purified prior to consumption.

TREATING WATER

Just because water is palatable (tastes good) does not mean that it is potable (safe to drink). All water should be considered in need of purification. There are many ways to purify water and you will find the most efficient ways of doing so listed below:

BOILING

This is the most preferred method of treating water. Bringing water to boiling point will kill 99.9 percent of parasites (including giardia and cryptosporidium). The giardia cyst dies at 60°C and cryptosporidium dies at 65°C. You must bring the water to a rolling boil before it is considered safe for human consumption. **Tip:** It is best to let water boil a full five minutes before letting it cool and drinking it.

CHEMICALS

Many chemicals can be utilized in the process of disinfecting water (see the following image for a few of the most common). In a survival situation, you may have to use what you have available. A good rule of thumb for exposure time and dosage is to double the dosage for turbid (cloudy) or cold water, double both the exposure time and dosage for water that is both turbid and cold when chlorine-based chemicals are used, and quadruple the time for iodine-based chemicals.

WATER PURIFICATION TABLETS

There are many different water purification tablets on the market today but dosages vary so you should follow the instructions written on the bottle.

Tip: You can use bleach to purify water by adding eight drops to each gallon of water or sixteen drops if the water is not clear. Shake well and let it sit for thirty minutes before drinking. You can do the same thing with tincture iodine by adding two drops per quart of water or ten drops if water is cloudy. Remember that some people are allergic to iodine, and it should never be used by women who are pregnant.

DISTILLATION

The distillation process involves capturing water just as it is transitioning from its gaseous form back into its liquid form. If you think about it from the perspective of rain, the sun heats the earth, which causes water to evaporate from the earth into a cloud,  which then returns to earth as 100 percent purified water that you can collect and drink without fear of contaminants. Examples of distillation are extracting dew on the morning grass by soaking it up with a cloth and ringing the cloth in your mouth or constructing a solar still that turns dirty water into gas and collecting it on a nonporous surface for consumption.

SOLAR ULTRAVIOLET LIGHT WATER DISINFECTION METHOD

The solar ultraviolet light water disinfection method uses the sun's rays to sterilize water and it will kill 99.9 percent of all viruses, bacteria, and protozoa that are present in the water. To use this method, you would put your water in a clear water container and then let it sit in the sunlight. This method requires 6 hours of direct sunlight for a liter of water to be purified. A much more accurate, effective, and rapid method of using UV rays to purify water is with a personal light pen which is small, lightweight, and it can purify a liter of water in 90 seconds.

WATER FILTERS

Water filters are a great way to filter out particulates from your water and to improve on its taste in order to make it more palatable, but that is where most "homemade" filters stop as far as protecting you from contaminants and waterborne disease. You can build a field expedient filtration device using dirt, leaves, pebbles, and ash layered into a plastic water bottle or sock. Manufactured water filters do a much better job of filtering water, even removing pathogens, but all filter elements and the gaskets that hold them in place eventu-ally erode with use, allowing

© Brian Morris

pathogens past the filter element, and there is typically no way to tell that this has happened unless you get sick. Microtubule filter technology is also very vulnerable to freezing, which can cause microfractures that allow pathogens to pass through the filter. Filtration can be used in conjunction with chemical water treatment but boiling is the preferred method of water treatment. All that said, it is far better to drink filtered water than to drink unfiltered water directly from the source when the purity levels are unknown.

ORAL REHYDRATION SOLUTION (ORS)

When you perspire, you lose electrolytes that are essential to life. It is also possible to flush electrolytes out of your system by drinking too much water. If you are lucky enough to have an oral rehydration solution packet in your EDC pack, use it to replace the loss of electrolytes in your body.

Tip: If you want to save money when preparing your EDC pack, you can make your own ORS by combining the following ingredients and then drinking it:

- 1 quart water
- ½ teaspoon baking soda
- 3 tablespoons sugar
- ½ teaspoon salt

Caution: Any of these ingredients can be eliminated except water! This solution can also be mixed more diluted than the yields listed above and still help, but ORS must not be mixed more concentrated than the yields listed above.

STORING WATER

There is a plethora of water storage techniques out there and they are only limited to one's imagination. In a wilderness survival situation, you may not have access to water storage gear such as a canteen or water bottle and it may become necessary to construct your own water storage container. Below are some examples of ways to do that:

WOODEN BOWL, CUP, OR BUCKET

Making a wooden bowl, cup, or bucket is simple, but it can be time-consuming. Start with a chunk of wood that is a few inches taller and wider than the depth you want your bowl, cup, or bucket to be. Next, center a pile of hot coals on top of your wood, about the circumference that you want the opening of your water container to be. Make sure you leave about an inch around the edge to keep the coals from burning through the wall of the vessel. Every ten minutes or so you want to remove the coals and use a scraping device such as a knife or stick to scrape away the charred area in the center of your wood block, creating a depression into the wood. Repeat these steps until the vessel is close to as deep as you want it. The final step is to scrape out the remainder of burned wood until the inside of the vessel is clear of the charred surface and unburned wood is visible. **Tip:** If you accidentally breach the side or bottom of the vessel, you can use tree sap to fill the hole and prevent the vessel from leaking.

BAMBOO SECTION
Bamboo is an abundant form of vegetation around the world. If you were to split a bamboo stalk sideways from top to bottom you would see that there are dividers separating the inside of a bamboo shoot into smaller compartments. If you cut the bamboo shoot into pieces and leave a divider as the base of the bamboo section, you will then have a vessel that you can store and transport water in. You can use a formed piece of wood or some cloth or even a large leaf to cover the container and prevent spillage.

LARGE LEAF/VEGETATION
A large leaf off a plant or tree has a nonporous surface and can be used for catching and collecting water.

ROCK DEPRESSION
Rock depressions, crevices, and other areas on a rock's surface where rainwater collects are generally pure, depending on your location. Water can be slurped up with your face, hands, or a straw.

TREE HOLLOW/STUMP
Tree hollows or stumps are excellent water collection sites, as crevices within wooden hollows/stumps hold rainwater that can be collected and consumed.

SEASHELL
Large seashells such as conch shells can be used for collecting and storing water.

TURTLE SHELL
You can use a turtle shell as a vessel to drink out of or, if large enough, for collecting rainwater.

SURVIVAL KIT
Inside of your survival kit you should have something to hold water in. You can use a plastic bag or even a nonlubricated condom.

PERSONAL HYDRATION SYSTEM
If you are prepared, you should have a personal hydration system such as a Camelbak® or similar hydration system that is capable of carrying at least two quarts of water.

WATER BOTTLE/CANTEEN/CANTEEN CUP

When venturing in the woods you should always carry an ample supply of water. Having a canteen or water bottle with a canteen cup will allow you to collect potentially contaminated water and then boil it in the canteen cup to render it purified. **Tip:** Plastic water bottles and other trash that you may find in the wilderness are survival "gold" and should never be discarded.

Caution: Water taken from rivers and other bodies of water known to have beavers likely contain traces of giardia and should always be brought to a rolling boil for 5 minutes prior to consumption.

Shelter

Mother Nature is the most powerful force on earth. Any person who recognizes and respects this fact will have a far greater chance of survival than those who choose to venture out into the wilderness unprepared. Keeping the body's core temperature stable in a survival situation is imperative, and that is why it is so important to find or construct an insulated shelter as soon as you realize you are in trouble.

The first consideration when constructing a shelter should be the size of your group. You should build your shelter to a size big enough to fit each person and their gear, but no bigger, and keep the ceiling low to increase heat retention. Avoid exposed hilltops, valley floors, moist ground, and avalanche paths. If you are in an area where there is snow, use it to create a

thermal barrier by applying six inches or so to the sides and roof of the shelter for additional heat conservation. Some other considerations should be how close your shelter site is to areas suitable for gathering firewood, how far your site is from a water source, and how far away your shelter would be from your signaling smoke fire (if you have one).

The shelter you choose should be simple enough to allow you to conserve energy, yet still meet your life essential needs such as keeping you warm and dry or cool and out of the sun. Remember, you can always build onto your existing shelter as time goes by if your survival strategy is to hold in place and wait to contact a rescue party.

Finally, you want to take into consideration what, if any, tools are available to you for building. The same thing goes for the shelter itself; you want to make sure there are ample natural resources available to you to build your survival shelter.

SHELTER BASICS

Any type of shelter, whether it is a permanent building, a tent, or an expedient shelter should meet six basic characteristics to be safe and effective:

1. **Protection from the elements:** The shelter must provide protection from rain, snow, wind, sun, etc.
2. **Heat retention:** It must have some type of insulation to retain heat; thus, preventing the waste of fuel.
3. **Ventilation:** Ventilation must be constructed, especially if burning fuel for heat. This prevents the accumulation of carbon monoxide as well as carbon dioxide (given off when breathing).
4. **Free from natural hazards:** Shelters should not be built in areas of avalanche hazards, under rock fall, or "standing dead" trees that have the potential to fall on your shelter.
5. **Stability:** Shelters must be constructed to withstand the pressures exerted by severe weather.
6. **Location:** Avoid exposed hilltops, valley floors, moist ground, and avalanche paths. Try to be within close proximity to firewood well as a water source. Ensure that your latrine area is not near your water source or to where you eat to prevent disease. Finally, you should face the opening of your shelter in the opposite direction from the prevailing wind to minimize wind damage.

PROTECTION FROM THE ELEMENTS

The shelter must provide protection from the elements. It needs to be free of natural hazards, such as large, dead tree branches or "widow makers" that could fall on your shelter and injure you or mud slides and rock falls that might be threats if your shelter is built at the base of a hill or cliff. Your shelter should be stable and strong enough to withstand the pressures exerted by severe weather. Wind and heavy rain or snow can put significant stresses on survival shelters and threaten their structural integrity. If your shelter won't last, neither will you. You should ensure that you are on a solid foundation and that you reinforce the framework with cordage, wire, or other means to enhance the stability of your shelter.

WAYS TO IMPROVE HEAT RETENTION

Another very important factor to take into consideration is heat retention. In colder climates you should insulate the outside of your survival shelter with all the materials you have available to use. After the framework, try to use a nonporous layer, such as a tarp, trash bags, or even large leaves that are layered like shingles over the framework. Then, use leaves and debris or even snow (an excellent insulator) to build up your outer shell and provide the maximum amount of warmth and heat retention.

VENTILATION CONSIDERATIONS

One feature often overlooked when constructing shelters is ventilation. You can quite easily die of carbon dioxide poisoning if you have no way of circulating fresh air into your shelter at all times. This is compounded when you burn fuel for heat or cooking inside your shelter, because it produces carbon monoxide, which is odorless and invisible and can also kill you quite rapidly if it's in a high enough concentration. Always be sure to create a ventilation hole that promotes a constant flow of fresh air to circulate inside your survival shelter. When time is a major factor, or if you just want to have a relatively safe place to base out of while you search for or construct a more efficient shelter, natural shelters such as caves or rock overhangs might be your best option. They are the easiest to establish and can be modified by laying walls of rocks, logs, or branches across the open sides. Hollow logs can be cleaned or dug out and then enhanced with a poncho, tarp, or pine boughs hung across the opening.

> **Caution:** One important point to be aware of is that natural shelters might already have "tenants" (snakes, bats, bears, mountain lions, rats, coyotes, or other animals) that will be reluctant to give up their home for you. Other concerns from animal residents include disease from decaying carcasses or animal scat.

NATURAL SHELTER PRECAUTIONS

Regardless of what type of shelter you decide to build, here are a few tips to apply to the design:

- Keep a low silhouette and reduce your living area to improve your heat retention.
- Avoid exposed hilltops, valley floors, moist ground, and mudslide and avalanche paths.
- Create a thermal barrier by applying snow, if available, to the shelter's roof and walls.
- Build your shelter in the vicinity of firewood, water, and signaling opportunities, if necessary.

There are many choices when it comes to what type of shelter to build in a survival situation. The best shelter is obviously a man-made permanent structure like a cabin or house that is built to take on the elements. Hunters' cabins are often made available in the more remote regions of the country for just such emergencies. You should always check with your local forest ranger station to find out the location of hunters' cabins and lean-to shelters in the vicinity of the area you are traveling through.

It is also advisable to always carry a fabricated survival shelter or a tent with you when traveling in the wilderness. If you do not have a tent and there are no man-made structures to be found, do a thorough reconnaissance of the area that you are in and try to find a cave or an ice cavern that you could improve with a few simple enhancements to protect you from the elements. Once you have exhausted your search for preexisting shelter and you have determined that there is none to be found, it is time to begin deciding on which style of survival shelter is best suited for the environment that you are in and what resources are available for you to construct your shelter. Note: Having a tarp or poncho with you can make all the difference when it comes to shelter construction. Not only can it be used as a nonporous material to keep your shelter dry and insulated, but it is also a shelter in its own right.

© Survivapedia

Caution: Natural shelters might appear stable but may be a trap waiting to collapse. Caves in mountainous regions may have natural gas pockets in them or may not have adequate ventilation. Fires may be built inside for heating or cooking but may be uncomfortable or even dangerous because of the smoke build-up.

In a winter survival situation, the shelter that probably stands out to most people is the igloo. But the fact is, an igloo is actually one of the hardest shelters to build in an emergency situation and requires the greatest level of skill and experience to construct. On top of that, it is also the most time-consuming shelter to build—and, when it comes to survival, time is your enemy.

When setting up shelter in winter environments you may choose to use a tent and that is totally acceptable as long as you winterize it to withstand wind, snow, and bone-chilling temperatures. There are several ways to winterize a tent that you can do individually or in unison. You can dig down to the ground or far enough that the depth coupled with a protective wall constructed with snow is enough to withstand wind and snow drifts, then pitch your tent on the surface of the ditch. Another technique is to reinforce your tent with an

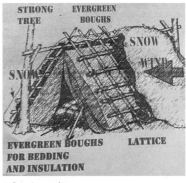

© Survivapedia

© Brian Morris

A-frame of sticks running vertically and horizontally, cover the framing with pine boughs or a like material, then shovel six inches to a foot of snow on top of that in order to create an effective protective barrier. Be sure to reinforce the front and back of the A-frame for added protection. If you need to make shelter during a thaw when the snow is slushy and the ground moist, a good technique is to use a platform of large branches or logs as the foundation of your shelter to keep you dry and warm.

SHELTER DESIGN

DEBRIS HUT

To build a debris hut, start by using either an existing deadfall tree or a long, strong, and straight branch with the bark shaved off to create a spine or ridge pole. The spine should be fixed at a 45° angle, with one end on the ground and the other end secured to the branch of another tree where it meets the trunk. You can also support the upper end by securing it atop the "V" notch created by lashing two additional branches together in the shape of an "A." The back of the shelter will be where the spine meets the ground, and the entrance will be where it is secured to the tree or V notch.

After the ribs are lashed in place, weave long sticks horizontally through the ribs to create a grid that will help support the weight of the outer layers of insulation. Next, lash the ribs onto the spine in a perpendicular manner from the spine, out at about 45 degrees to the ground. Position the ribs as close to one another as possible because this will make insulating and waterproofing much easier.

Once the skeleton is finished, the next step is to waterproof the structure. You can do this by securing a tarp or poncho over the top of the spine and the ribs to make more of a traditional-looking tent. If you don't have those items, you can weave large leaves, greenery, or pine boughs, as well as any other leafy debris into the ribs to keep snow and rain out. Weave brush into the ribs to hold your greenery in place. Add branches with green leaves (shiny side up). After this, you can pile on debris and/or snow to finish the insulation process. Once you have filled all the gaps, you can put a layer of pine needles on top for added insulation. If it has snowed, consider making the final layer of your shelter out of snow, because it is an outstanding insulator.

> **Tip:** Roofing materials should be laid down like shingles from the bottom up so that rainwater can't penetrate under the roofing materials and into the shelter.

SAPLING SHELTER

This type of shelter can be constructed in an area where an abundance of saplings is growing. Find or clear an area so that you have two parallel rows of saplings at least 4' long and approximately 1½'–2' apart. Bend the saplings together and tie them to form several hoops which will form the framework of the shelter. Next, cover the hoops with a water-repellent covering. The shelter then may be insulated with

© Survivapedia

leaves, brush, snow, or boughs. Finally, close one end permanently. Hang material over the other end to form a door.

LEAN-TO

A lean-to can be built in heavily forested areas and requires a limited amount of cordage to construct. The lean-to is an effective shelter but does not offer a great degree of protection from the elements. Select a site with two trees (4"–12" in diameter), spaced far enough apart that a man can lie

down between them. Two sturdy poles can be substituted by inserting them into the ground at the proper distance apart. Cut a pole to support the roof. It should be at least 3"–4" in diameter and long enough to extend 4"–6" past both trees. Tie the pole horizontally between the two trees, approximately 1 yard off the deck. Then, cut several long poles to be used as stringers. Place them along the horizontal support bar approximately every 1½' and laid on the ground. All stringers may be tied to or laid on the horizontal support bar. A short wall of rocks or logs may be constructed on the ground to lift the stringers off the ground, creating additional height and living room dimensions. Finally, cut several saplings and weave them horizontally between the stringers. Cover the roof with water-repellent and insulating material.

FALLEN TREE BIVOUAC

The fallen tree bivouac is an excellent shelter because most of the work has already been done. First, ensure the tree you're going to use is stable prior to constructing. Start by cutting away branches on the underside to make a hollow underneath. Place additional insulating material to the top and sides of the tree. Once you have sealed the top and sides with waterproofing and insulating materials, your shelter is complete.

© Survivapedia

TEEPEE SURVIVAL SHELTER

The teepee-style survival shelter is an excellent choice whenever three pole-like sticks, some cordage, and some sort of nonporous materials are available. It should be noted that a traditional teepee is far more complicated to build than the shelter being described here. That said, the basic advantages of a teepee are still incorporated into

this teepee-style shelter design. Once you have the items listed above, the first thing you want to do is make sure your three poles are long enough to build a fire inside without setting the shelter on fire. One of the biggest advantages of the teepee-style shelter is the exhaust opening in the shelter. This coupled with the height of the shelter make it possible to build a small fire inside of the teepee which gives you maximum heat retention and the ability to keep your fire burning through inclement weather conditions.

Start by laying your poles side by side. Then, lash all poles together about six to twelve inches down from the tops of the poles, bunch all of your poles together, and make multiple wraps around the entire bundle with the remainder of the courage you used to lash the poles when they were side by side.

Next, stand up your poles and spread them out evenly spaced in the shape of a tripod. If you are using poles that are larger and heavier at one end, be sure to use that end as the bottom side of the pole in order to increase stability of the structure. If you have additional natural resources available, you can improve on the frame of your teepee by adding additional vertical poles and/or sticks as horizontal support between poles. Be sure to shave off any sharp ends on any of your support sticks or poles so as not to tear into the material you are using to waterproof the teepee.

Once you have done all you can to create a sturdy frame, the next step is to waterproof and insulate your teepee survival shelter. You can use animal hides, a tarp, ponchos, or any other water-resistant materials that will keep the rain, snow, and wind out of your shelter, retain heat, and provide protection from the sun in the hotter months.

Using your cordage to secure the tarp or other water-resistant materials in place, wrap around the poles as tight as possible, then either stake down the tarp or water-resistant materials or use rocks and logs to hold down the bottom.

SWAMP BED SHELTER

A swamp bed is nothing more than a platform that is raised off the ground. Any time you are in an environment where you need to be elevated above the ground and there are trees or deadfall wood as an available resource, the swamp bed is a good shelter for you. To build a swamp bed, start by building the legs. Find four trees that are in the vicinity of where you want your swamp bed and are growing in the four corners of a rectangular or square shape that is the length and width that you want your swamp bed to be. You would then need to find four sticks that are sturdy enough to hold the weight of you and all of your gear without bending or breaking. Lash your horizontal framing sticks to the vertical supporting trees one at a time at the desired height off the ground until the frame of your platform is secured above the ground. The final step is to gather enough sticks to cover the surface of the platform when laid side by side from one end to the other. Try to ensure that these sticks are as close to equal in diameter as you can find, then shave them smooth until they are free of nubs and sharp splinters. It's advisable to either lash down the ends of the platform sticks or, for a more secure hold, lay a stick vertically over each side of the platform and lash the stick down to keep the ends of the platform sticks from coming up. Do the same thing on the opposite side of the platform.

If you can't find four trees positioned in such a way that provides simple support legs for your swamp bed, or if you want to construct a swamp bed

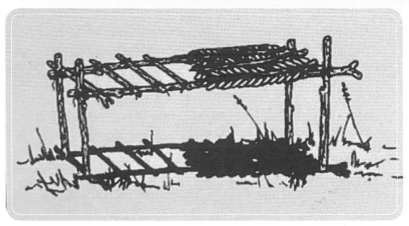

© US Army

that is transportable and that you can take with you when you move position and camp sites, you can do this easily by constructing portable supporting legs. To do this, build the platform in the same manner as previously described but instead of lashing the platform to four trees, lash it to itself as a stand-alone legless platform. Then, gather twelve sturdy sticks thick enough in diameter to be capable of supporting all the weight you plan on the platform supporting. To begin, take three of the sticks and lay them evenly side by side, then lash them together a little shy of a third of the way down from the top. Spread the sticks into the form of a tripod. Repeat this process three more times for a total of four tripods. Place a tripod under each corner of the platform to raise it above the ground. You can make more tripods as needed for added support.

SAND DUNE SHELTER

Being able to successfully construct a shelter in a desert environment can be the difference between life and death in this extremely unforgiving landscape and climate zone. While desert temperatures vary greatly based on the time of year and their geo-location, temperatures can range from highs up to 140°F to lows down to 100°F below zero. The average temperature in the desert is 110°F during the day and 50°F at night. These extreme temps and the fact that 33 percent of the earth's land mass is desert are great reasons to become educated on how to build a survival shelter in this harsh environment.

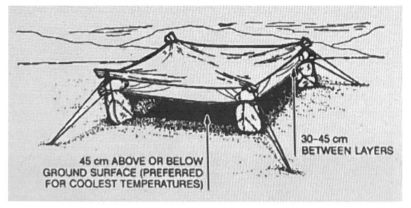

45 cm ABOVE OR BELOW GROUND SURFACE (PREFERRED FOR COOLEST TEMPERATURES)

30–45 cm BETWEEN LAYERS

© US Army

Always avoid working or exerting energy during the heat of the day. All of your movements and physical exertions should be aimed toward the early morning before the sun gets too high or in the evening when the air and sand begin to cool.

Site selection for your desert shelter is crucial. The best location would be someplace like the backside of a sand dune where it would be feasible for you to dig a trench. If there are rocks in the area along with the soft sand, even better. Dig a trench about 2 feet deep and as wide and long as you need to comfortably fit yourself and your gear.

The next thing you want to do is to build walls around your ditch from 2–3 feet high using sand, rocks, clay, and any other natural materials you have. Be sure to leave an opening big enough for you to get in and out of. Make sure to leave it on the side of the ditch that is in the opposite direction of prevailing wind.

Finally, you need to construct your roof. Preferably, you would want a thick tarp or canvas cover for a roof but any material that will either partially or completely block the harmful rays of the sun will be better than no cover at all.

In a true emergency life-and-death survival situation your imagination is essential in getting you the things that you need to survive in this sparse environment. You can use clothing, a poncho, a space blanket, materials from an abandoned vehicle, or even natural materials such as plants, cactus skin, or tumbleweeds to cover your shelter.

Remember, in the harsh desert environment all creatures are on a constant search for reprieve from the rays of the relentless sun so be sure to do a thorough check of the inside of your desert survival shelter for wildlife that may have crawled in uninvited every time before entering.

SNOW MOUND SHELTER

© Survivapedia

There are many different techniques to construct a snow mound shelter. The simplest way to do it is to find a preformed snow cave and improve on it to become your shelter. If you can't find a snow cave, look for a hard-packed snow drift. On the opposite side of the direction of the prevailing wind, begin to dig out a cave just large enough to hold you and your gear. You can use your backpack or some pine boughs to create a makeshift door. Once you finish your shelter, you should carve out or construct an elevated sleeping platform so that you are as close to the warm air at the top of the shelter.

Another technique for building a snow mound is to pile snow as high as you can and pack it down into as tight packed of a mound as you can get it. After allowing for the packed snow to harden, proceed in the same manner as you would when digging into a snow drift. Snow caves and snow mound shelters can be heated by a single candle, which will raise the inside temperature anywhere from 5°F–15°F.

Caution: A ventilation hole is a particularly vital feature in any snow shelter since snow is nonporous and does not allow dirty carbon-filled air out or clean oxygen-rich air in. A ventilation hole should be dug through the roof at a 45° angle above the entrance. A ski pole or branch should be left in the hole to mark the hole and allow clearing should the ventilation hole become clogged. A pine bough branch can be placed into the outside of the roof above the hole to aid in keeping the hole clear during falling snow. If a candle is left burning while individuals sleep, someone should stay awake to ensure that the air hole stays open in order to reduce the danger of asphyxiation.

CAVE

A cave can be an outstanding survival shelter, but this fact does not always go unnoticed by the local wildlife, so make sure that the cave you intend to use for shelter is empty or at least free of any wild guests that can do you harm.

Tip: You can burn wet wood to smoke out most unwanted guests from a cave.

SNOW CAVE

Similar to an igloo, a snow cave is an outstanding way to protect yourself from the cold and windchill in a survival situation. Snow caves that were built by animals for these same reasons can be found in the wild. Humans can use these shelters if they find them but there is a good chance that the snow cave is inhabited so you will need to make sure that it is safe to enter before doing so.

If you cannot find an animal-made snow cave, you can build one yourself. It will help if you can locate a snowdrift, as that will give you a compacted pile of snow to begin with. On the opposite side of the drift from the prevailing wind, dig an opening big enough for you and your gear to get inside comfortably. You can use a chunk of snow or your gear to close the opening of the snow cave after construction. It's extremely important to have good ventilation when constructing a snow cave, as snow is a nonporous substance that will not allow carbon dioxide to escape and can be extremely dangerous or deadly.

> **Caution:** Be sure to ventilate your snow cave. If the carbon dioxide in the cave is not allowed to escape and fresh air is not able to enter, it can be a deadly combination. Carbon dioxide will build up inside the cave, and since this substance has no smell and is not visible to the human eye, the habitant of the cave will not realize what is happening and can easily drift off into unconsciousness and die.

TENT

One of the best ways to protect your-self from the elements when venturing out into the wilderness is to have a tent that is designed for the environment that you are in. Some tents are designed for specific seasons, so you want to make sure that you either carry a four-season tent or a tent that is rated

for the time of year that you are out in the wild. You can use natural materials to reinforce your tent and make it much more insulated but remember that if you do this you will need to establish a means of ventilation, as the ventilating properties that come in tents will be lost if they are covered with natural brush or snow. It is best to start by building a wooden frame around your tent to hold the weight of whatever natural materials you plan to put on the outside of your tent for insulation.

PONCHO SHELTER

This is one of the easiest shelters to construct. Materials needed for construction are cord and any water-repellent material such as a poncho or tarp. It should be one of the first types of shelter considered if planning a short stay in any one place. To build this shelter, simply secure each corner of your pon-

cho or other nonporous material to a tree just about two feet off the ground. Next, secure the top of your poncho at the center with cordage and tie it to a branch or to something directly above the shelter so that the covering takes on the look of a circus tent. Then, use dirt, sand, pine needles, leaves, or whatever other materials you can find to close off the sides and back of the shelter. Finally, you can use pine needles or whatever other debris are in the area to create a warm insulator between you and the ground.

SURVIVAL SHELTER BED

No matter what kind of survival shelter you choose to build, you will need something to sleep on. Lying directly on the ground is dangerous for multiple reasons. It can easily drain all the heat from your body quite quickly and it leaves you susceptible to getting wet, to insects and other animals, and to impeding rest and sleep, which is essential to have in a survival scenario. The two easiest beds you can build are stick beds and leaf beds.

STICK BED

To build a stick bed, start by laying down three straight sticks that are each about the same diameter. Make sure the sticks you choose are as long as you want the length of your bed to be. Place one base stick on the left edge of the bed, one on the right, and one in the middle. Use wooden stakes to pin the  three base sticks in place, then gather enough sticks to lay across the three base sticks perpendicular to the three base sticks with several inches of overhang on each side. Finally, use sharpened wooden stakes to pin each end of the bed in place, leaving several inches above the height of the base sticks, then lay down the surface sticks side by side from one end of the bed to the other.

LEAF BED

To build a leaf bed, the first thing you want to do is build the frame. Start by gathering enough straight branches that are about a foot longer than the length of your body and measure up to about a foot high when stacked one on top of the other. Next, drive in two side-by-side stakes far enough apart to fit  the widest branch that you gathered, then do the exact same thing on the opposite end of the bed, leaving just over a foot of stake out of the ground.

Lay your straight sticks in between the stakes on either side of the bed, one on top of the other until you have a retaining wall that is about a foot high. Repeat this process on the other side of the bed's width until you have two retaining walls running parallel to each other and as wide apart as you desire the width of your bed to be. Make sure that you leave about one foot of the locking stake above the ground. The next step is to repeat this entire process at the head and foot of the bed using sticks that are one foot longer than the width of the bed. At this point you should have a retaining wall the shape of a rectangle with one-foot-high walls all around. The final step is to construct your "mattress." Simply fill the walled frame with leaves, pine needles, and other soft debris from the forest floor. It is advisable to lie on the bed and roll left and right several times as you fill it to ensure that everything is packed down nicely.

FIRE WALL (WIND BLOCKER)

There are many reasons that you may need to build a simple wall in a survival scenario. The two most common reasons would be to reflect the heat of your fire back into your survival shelter and to protect you and your fire from being affected by the wind. Making a wall is a relatively simple thing to do in most environments if you take advantage of all of the available natural resources. In

© Survivapedia

snow and arctic regions where trees and sticks may not be readily available, it is possible to use snow and ice as a protective wall. In arid desert regions, you can use rocks and sand to create a protective barrier.

To make a fire wall in a woodland environment, start by gathering enough straight branches that are about a foot longer than the length that you want your protective wall to be and measure up to about three to four feet high when stacked one on top of the other. Next, find four stakes about one and a half feet longer than the desired height of your wall and sharpen one end of each to allow ease of driving them into the ground. Use a rock, bat-like stick, or any other hammer-like tool to drive in two side-by-side stakes about a foot and a half deep and far enough apart to fit your widest branch that you gathered. Repeat this process with the other two stakes on the opposite side of the wall. Lay your wall sticks one by one in between the two stakes on one side of the wall and then the other. Continue to stack sticks one on top of the other until you have built up your wall to the desired height. It is not always necessary, but it can be helpful to reinforce your walls with mud, sand, and dirt to fill in the gaps and provide more insulation from the elements.

"CAT HOLE" FIELD LATRINE

Field hygiene is paramount in a survival situation. Even in bushcrafting, where you are intentionally spending extended periods of time out in the wilderness, make sure to keep clean and designate a field latrine two hundred feet away from your shelter and/or water source.

What you'll need:
- Shovel
- Toilet paper (leaves work just fine but make sure you identify them as nonpoisonous first!)
- Hand sanitizer

Where to go:
- Two hundred feet from your campsite or any water source

What to do:
1. Dig a hole one foot wide by one foot deep
2. Do your business (you can dig a deeper 2–3-foot hole and build a seat as depicted in the photo)
3. Fill in hole with dirt
4. Wash your hands thoroughly

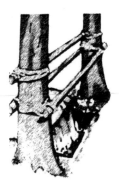

© Survivapedia

Caution: Take particular care to adequately cover urine and feces with dirt or lime and dirt or to simply collect all of your waste in a plastic bag and pack it out to prevent it from being spread by wild animals and flies and possibly contaminating drinking water or food.

Security

In the modern world the human is the apex predator among all animals big and small. Instead of sharp teeth and long claws, we've evolved in such a way that we are able to use the grey matter between our ears (some more than others) to defend ourselves and as weapons of war through superior strategy and thought coupled with hand-eye coordination, and the somewhat unique ability to use our opposable thumbs and dexterity to build weapons if we can't effectively get the job done with our bare hands. All this being said, it is also important to remember that humans are social animals, and we are genetically programmed to work as a team even when we fight. Unfortunately, it does not always work out this way and we are not always accompanied by other able-bodied fighters every time danger lurks out in the wilderness.

When you hear about someone being killed in the wilderness or ocean (or even lakes, streams, and rivers) it is almost always a case where they put themselves into a situation where they were either imitating the actions of the prey or appearing to threaten the offspring of another apex predator that shared the habitat and territory they were in. The best thing you can do in a bushcraft survival scenario when there are other apex predators sharing the same airspace as you is to have a healthy respect for these animals and maintain enough distance between you and the animal to give yourself time to react if the animal decides to attack you.

It also pays to learn about the hunting, feeding, and defense behaviors of these animals, as this knowledge can surely save your life. Whatever you do, stay away from cute and curious apex predator offspring like tiger, lion, or bear cubs as they are a sure way to piss off mom and give you more excitement than you may be able to handle. Ambush predators like alligators and crocodiles that lie in wait on grassy riverbanks to attack when prey animals come in for a drink are another predator that you should be aware of when in their habitat.

Other things to consider in a bushcraft survival situation are how you store food. Many animals have incredible senses of smell and will vector in on your camp and maybe even on you within seconds of spilling the blood of your catch. Bears have amazing olfactory sense, so sites should be broken up into sleeping, cooking/eating/food and trash storage, and hygiene areas laid out in a triangle with a minimum of one hundred meters distance between the three areas. Bears will smell areas where you relieve yourself, prepare game, cook, eat, and store food, so placing these areas far from where you sleep reduces the chances that a bear will catch you sleeping. Set perimeter alarms in all areas.

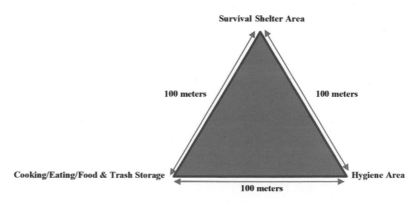

© Brian Morris

In the area for cooking/eating/food and trash storage, store food in scent-proof bags if possible and hang your food by running a slick line over a branch high in a tree. Also consider these factors when setting and surviving traps and snares, as the cries of wounded prey that you have trapped can easily call other apex creatures such as bears, packs of wild dogs, coyotes, or even wolves depending on where you are located.

Security is having the peace of mind to know that you have done everything possible to prepare for a survival scenario and that you have mitigated all the risks involved in whatever dangerous or potentially dangerous activities you are participating in. In this chapter we will go over some tried-and-true Green Beret tricks to moving in a stealthy and tactical manner and setting up a defensive perimeter when you are not moving so that you are ready for whatever comes your way. Situational awareness, understanding your operational environment, and remaining vigilant to solid security practices are the foundation of all Special Operations methods and tactics. In a wilderness survival scenario, putting these practices into action can definitely give you the tactical advantage if you apply them to every decision you make.

> **Tip:** This Special Forces adage never gets old: "Proper Prior Planning Prevents Piss Poor Performance!"

MOVEMENT IN UNFAMILIAR TERRAIN

Whether you are moving or sitting still you should *always* have 360-degree security if possible. It takes a minimum of two people to maintain 360-degree security with one covering from 9:00 a.m. to 3:00 p.m. and the other covering from 3:00 p.m. to 9:00 a.m. (thus the saying "I got your six," meaning "I have your back"). If

it's just you, obviously you can't see behind yourself, and even if there are only two of you and one is always awake, that person can't see behind himself either. That's why the less people you have the more important it is to keep good cover and concealment to your back and all around you. You want to be as hidden as possible while still allowing for observation of any key avenues of approach and you want to always plan for an escape route in case your position is compromised. Another good rule of thumb is to practice "security halts" periodically in order to get used to different terrains and environments as you move along a route and to get familiar with the sights, sounds, and smells of the area you are in.

DEFENDING YOURSELF

No matter if it is an apex predator that is stalking you or a large animal that you are attempting to dispatch for food, good security practices will be vital to mitigating the chances of your becoming wounded or worse in such a scenario. By applying the following three principals to your planning and execution process, you can greatly enhance your chances of success:

> **Speed:** Speed is the momentum that carries the survivor and helps them take the most advantage in the first few surprise seconds. Speed becomes security for the survivor.
>
> **Surprise:** Surprise is the key to any assault. Catching a threat by surprise will give the survivor the initial advantage by throwing the threat off guard, thereby giving the survivor the tactical advantage.
>
> **Violence of action:** Violence of action is sudden and explosive force. It can instill the threat with fear and confusion and greatly improve the survivor's chances of quickly dispatching the threat.

> **Caution:** It should be noted that in a survival situation you should try to avoid conflict whenever possible, as even a small and seemingly minimal wound can become debilitating or even catastrophic in the absence of immediate medical attention.

WEAPONS

If you find yourself in a wilderness survival scenario, one of your first priorities should be to put your firearm into its ready configuration so that you have it available should a threat present itself. In the event that you do not have a firearm with you, you should construct a weapon immediately with whatever materials are available to you.

© Brian Morris

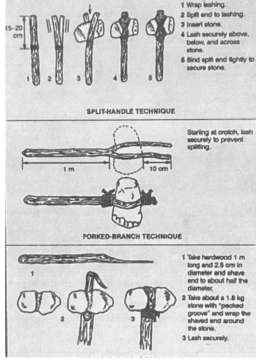

1 Wrap lashing.
2 Split end to lashing.
3 Insert stone.
4 Lash securely above, below, and across stone.
5 Bind split end tightly to secure stone.

15-20 cm

SPLIT-HANDLE TECHNIQUE

1 m   10 cm

Starting at crotch, lash securely to prevent splitting.

FORKED-BRANCH TECHNIQUE

1 Take hardwood 1 m long and 2.5 cm in diameter and shave end to about half the diameter.

2 Take about a 1.8 kg stone with "pecked groove" and wrap the shaved end around the stone.

3 Lash securely.

© US Army

FIREARMS

When it comes to firearms, in a survival situation, any firearm that you have is better than no firearm at all. That said, certain types of firearms can be more advantageous than others in a perfect world. Pistols are great because they are small enough to keep on your body at the ready at all times, but they can lack the stopping power of certain apex predators, depending on caliber.

© Brian Morris

Rifles give the survivor the advantage of stand-off, meaning they allow the survivor to kill the threat from great distance which lowers the chances of a "face-to-face" conflict with a threat. A .22 caliber is great because it can be utilized by the survivor for everything from food procurement to self-defense. Taking the survival scenario into consideration when choosing a weapon to keep in your EDC pack, the shotgun is probably the most versatile firearm you can have, as it offers the survivor the ability to transition from slugs for long distance to buck, bird shot, and even flare rounds for rescue signaling. At the end of the day, the weapon you have with you or lack thereof is completely up to the survivor. If you carry a firearm with you whenever possible you greatly increase the chances of having one with you when and if you find yourself in a wilderness survival scenario.

> **Tip:** What is the best weapon to have in a survival situation? The answer is the one you have with you.

BEAR SPRAY

Bear spray is a nonlethal weapon that can be used to disorient an attacking threat. It will cause severe irritation to the eyes and cause the threat to tear up. Bear spay can also burn exposed skin or cause significant irritation. If bear spray is inhaled, it will more than likely cause coughing or sneezing and in  some cases the threat may back off from its attack or disengage completely and search for a less threatening target. That said, never conclude that the attack is over just because the threat is temporarily disabled. Once they recover, they may resume the attack unless you are able to use that time to escape or neutralize the threat.

SURVIVAL KNIFE

A knife is by far one of the most important and versatile survival tools that you can have and hope- fully, if nothing else, you have made it a priority to carry a good knife with you at all times without fail. The two basic types of knives are folding and fixed blade. Fixed blade knives are stored in a sheath.

© Brian Morris

The best fixed blade knives have a "full tang," meaning they are made from one piece of metal running from the tip of the blade to the base of the handle and tend to be stronger than folding models or fixed blades that do not have a full tang. Folding knives can be easily broken no matter what the manufacturer claims, however they are much easier to carry and therefore are more likely to be on your person when and if you find yourself in an emergency survival situation. When choosing a survival knife, look for one with a good quality blade and a sharp point that is durable enough to dig with if necessary. It should also feel comfortable in your hand and have a durable handle.

IMPROVISED WEAPONS

Never pass up the opportunity to arm yourself the moment you find yourself in a wilderness survival situation. Since firearms are not likely to be loaded at your feet for you to pick up and use, you are going to have to think outside the box if you're going to have a chance at protecting yourself and your loved ones. There are many good weapons that our ancestors used to defend themselves and their families. The fact is, anything that you can use to harm or kill another living creature is considered a weapon. Weapons serve a dual purpose. You use them to obtain and prepare food and to provide self-defense. A weapon can also give you a feeling of security and provide you with the ability to hunt on the move. If you do not have a weapon with you such as a firearm or knife, it will be necessary for you to make a field expedient or improvised weapon with whatever materials you can find. Here are a few ideas that you can use or improve on if you ever find yourself in need of arming yourself to stay alive:

SIMPLE SPEAR

Making a spear is simple. Start by finding a long pull hardwood stick small enough in diameter to fit comfortably in your hand but wide enough that it can withstand the pressure of thrusting it into another ani-  mal. You want the stick to be about a third taller than you are. Make sure that it is made from hardwood. Once you have found your spear stick, shave off all of the twigs and nubs until you have one smooth pole that is about the same diameter at the top as it is at the bottom. The next step is to begin to sharpen one end of the spear, leaving the bottom end of the spear blunt. Once you have brought the spear's tip to a sharp point you want to carefully lay the tip of the spear above a hot fire or coals and slowly rotate it, being careful not to burn beyond the outer surface of the wood. The idea is that the heat from the fire will harden the wood, making it far less likely to break or dull during use.

> It is best to use live or recently cut wood for use as a spear, as older wood will easily snap or crack. Additionally, try to use wood that is thick enough that it won't bend when it has pressure applied to it.

SPEAR WITH STONE/BONE SPEARHEAD

The initial process of making a spear with a stone or bone spearhead is exactly the same as that of making a wooden spear with a carved head. Once you have selected and prepared the piece of wood that you're going to use as your spear pole and you have hardened the top of the pole in a fire, *do not* continue carving one end of the spear to a point. Instead, split the wood down the center of one end of the spear about four to six inches down.

Find a thin piece of rock that is chipped, carved, or fashioned into a pointed spearhead. If you can, carve or chip a V notch into the bottom of the spearhead about as wide as the diameter of the pole; this will help give the spearhead a tighter and more secure fit onto the spear pole. Make sure that whatever material you're using as a spearhead is as flat as possible so that it will fit snugly between the split wood of your spear. Take the spearhead and place it into the split at the top of the spear pole and push it down so that there is enough wood left above the spearhead to lash together and hold the spearhead in place. You also want to lash directly below the spearhead, as this will keep the wood from continuing to split and possibly break off and it will further tighten and secure the spearhead in place onto your spear pole. If possible, you can further secure the spearhead by continuing to lash the bottom end of the stone or rock spearhead to the pole.

Tip: Use green/live wood as your weapon handle, as it will allow you to bend the weapon around after splitting it.

SIMPLE CLUB

A simple club needs to be long enough to do major damage to whatever you are swinging it at and short enough that you can easily swing it with one arm. You want the club to be heavy  and strong enough that it will not break on contact with whatever you are hitting.

WEIGHTED CLUB

The weighted club is much like a simple club except for the fact that there is something heavy at the business end of the club. This object could be a natural knot that is part of the wood club itself or it could be a heavy object that you lashed to the end of the club in the same fashion that you lashed the spearhead to the spear above.

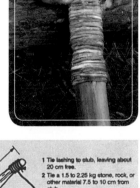

SWING CLUB

To make a swing club, start by finding a short club at a size that fits snugly in your hand. This club should feel a lot like a baseball bat when held. Using your knife, cut a notch completely around the circumference of the top of the club that is a few inches down from the tip and wide enough for the girth of your cordage to sit nicely into the notch to prevent it from slipping up and down. Tie one end of your

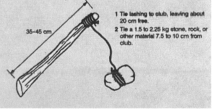

© US Army

cordage tightly to the club, seating the cord into the notch before tying or lashing the rope in place. On the business end the rope, lash and tie on a heavy object that is around the size of a baseball. The length of your rope only needs to be about eight inches long. Any longer and there is a good chance that you will hit yourself with the rock when twirled or swung. The idea is that the addition of the flexible cordage and heavy object to the end of the club multiplies the force of the club considerably. There is also the added benefit of giving yourself a bit more stand-off distance from whatever you are trying to beat to death than you would get with a simple club alone.

BATTLE HAMMER/BATTLE AXE

A battle hammer is a great weapon to defend yourself with against most threats if constructed and used properly. Think of it like a baseball bat on steroids. It makes for a great weapon when blunt force trauma is your intention. Another variation of this weapon is the battle axe. To make a battle axe, you will want to find a stone that you can flake and chip to a sharp edge. Structurally, a battle hammer and/ or battle axe is not too much different than any of the other weapons that require you to lash a stone into a split piece of green wood. Once you have selected and prepared the piece

of wood that you are going to use as your battle axe handle, split the wood down the center of the top end of the handle and far enough down to bend both sides of the split wood around the rock you are using as your axe head or hammerhead. Make sure you leave a few inches above the rock head to allow you to tie it tight above the head of the weapon. Once the axe or hammer is set in place, use whatever cordage or lashing materials you have to lash the head firmly in place onto the handle.

STONE KNIFE

To make a stone knife, you will need a sharp-edged piece of stone, a chipping tool, and a flaking tool. A chipping tool is a light, blunt-edged tool used to break off small pieces of stone. A flaking tool is a pointed tool used to break off thin, flattened pieces of stone. You can

make a chipping tool from wood, bone, or metal, and a flaking tool from bone, antlers, or soft iron. Lash the blade to some type of handle.

Note: Stone will make an excellent puncturing tool and a good chopping tool but will not hold a fine edge. Some stones such as chert or flint can have very fine edges.

BONE KNIFE

Bone knives work excellently as puncturing weapons but they will not hold an edge and could flake and shatter easily if used improperly. Start with the leg bone of a medium to large animal such as a deer. Place the bone on a flat stone and use a rock to slam down on the bone and fragment into pieces. Pick up the piece that is best suited for you to use as a puncturing knife and, using a coarse rock, continue by rubbing the bone with the rock on the flat stone until all the fragments are sanded down and the bone comes to a smooth point.

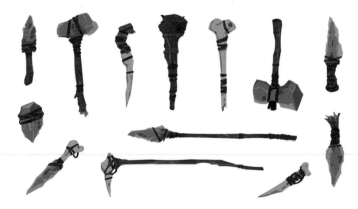

WOOD KNIFE

The only wood that will hold an edge is bamboo. If you do not have bamboo and are working with any other type of wood, you will have to make your knife into a puncturing weapon. Start by grinding the wood down to a sharp point on a coarse rock. The next thing you want to do is to fire-

harden the point in much the same way you would with a spear by drying the blade or point of the knife over the fire slowly until it is slightly charred. The drier you make the wood, the harder the point will be.

> **Tip:** Use only the straight-grained portions of the wood. Do not use the core or pith, as it will make a weak point.

ARROWHEAD

Making an effective arrowhead requires some skill but it can be done if you have the time and are able to practice. Like most wilderness survival skills, you are much better off if you learn them prior to an emergency occurring. To make an arrowhead, use a rock that chips easily such as flint and a harder rock  as a knapping tool to chip away at the flint. Once you have knapped off a thin, sharp flake of flint, refine it with a smaller tool that will allow you to knap the flint into the shape of arrowhead you desire. A multi-tool or even a piece of deer antler or bone works well for this.

WAR CLUB OR BATTLE AXE

War clubs can make for highly effective field expedient weapons when constructed and employed correctly. To construct a war club, simply find a piece of natural material about the length of a baseball bat that is strong enough to swing and strike a threat without the club breaking.

You can improve on your war club by turning it into a battle axe. To do this, simply split the top of the club in half (on the top end only), then wedge in a sharp or blunt object such as a stone in between the split wood. Finally, lash the split wood around the object to secure it in place.

EARLY WARNING SYSTEMS AND SETTING UP A DEFENSIVE PERIMETER

Even in a survival scenario, you have to eat and sleep, and you may not have anyone with you to watch your back when doing so. In order to maintain security when your guard is down or when you are concentrating on other priorities of work, you can set up a defensive perimeter and utilize early warning systems to give you a heads-up that there may be a threat approaching that requires your attention.

TRIP WIRE

You can use any cordage or string as a trip wire to initiate a commercially made or field expedient early warning system or device. To construct a trip wire, start by identifying a likely path or trail that runs into your bivouac location. Tie one end of the trip wire to a tree, then secure the other end to your triggering system. Depending on what materials you have with you, the trigger can be anything from the pull ring of a pyrotechnic device to a simple rock balanced delicately in an elevated position so that it will fall, strike another rock slab, and make a loud noise to alert you to a possible threat. To most successfully provide yourself with an effective 360-degree early warning system, you should interlock these trip wire systems all around your static location.

SETTING UP A DEFENSIVE PERIMETER

To set up a defensive perimeter around your bivouac position, utilize any materials you can find to create a wall-like barrier around your static location. It is best to use sticks that are thick enough to deter a threat from walking over or through. Whenever possible, you should try to add briars and thorny brush in your walls to add to its deterrence abilities.

> **Note:** Make sure you provide yourself with an easily identifiable escape route, as you don't want to find yourself trapped inside your own perimeter.

FIRE STICK

Most animals that pose a danger to humans will at least take caution at the sight of fire and at best will stand clear of it. The sight and smell of a fire can travel great distance so in a survival situation it can't hurt to always have a fire going when you are in a stationary position. If you have some material like cloth from a shirt you can wrap it around the end of a stick to create a torch. You can also use flammable oils such as bug repellant or other flammable liquids to saturate the end of the torch prior to use. To employ the torch, pick up the stick and (if available)

saturate the end of the stick with a flammable substance. Being careful not to burn yourself, either use one of your fire-starting tools such as a lighter or hold the torch over an existing fire until it ignites. You now have a long stick with a burning tip to swing at and hopefully ward off a wild animal.

> **Tip:** If you use a spear as a torch, you have an additional weapon to fall back on if the fire does not scare off the predator. Use the blunt end of the spear as the torch so as not to burn the hardened spear tip.

LIONS, TIGERS, BEARS, AND OTHER APEX PREDATORS

Ideally, one should never venture out into the wilderness without knowing exactly which apex predators are living in the area. People are often caught off guard by bears, mountain lions, and other wildlife seen within miles or less of areas highly populated by humans. This is why it is so important to learn everything you can about the apex predators that could be looking at you as potential prey were you to be stranded in the wilderness with nothing to protect you and no place to provide you with protection from these animals.

Not all apex creatures are designed to run after their prey. Some, like alligators and crocodiles, can be ambush predators, waiting patiently for their unsuspecting prey to drop down for a drink of water where they use their ability to strike out lighting fast and clamp down on their kill with amazing, bone-crushing force. Knowing how each one of these animals hunt their prey will keep you one step ahead of them and give you the ability to either put distance between you and them or give you a fighting chance at protecting yourself and anyone you are with. It is said that a polar bear can smell blood from twenty miles away.

Don't let ignorance turn you into just another statistic. When traveling, particularly through remote locations, do a good study of the natural environments that you will potentially be traveling through and have a solid understanding of all the threats that you may have to face were you to be stranded and on your own.

Communications and Emergency Signal Techniques

O ne of the first things you should try to do in a survival situation is start thinking about how you can signal for other people to help you get out of the situation that you are in. The first step to communication in a survival situation is to get the attention of someone who can rescue or assist you.

In this chapter, you will learn ways to signal for rescue, including radios and International Morse Code. You will also learn about electronic signaling devices including strobe lights, personal locator beacons (PLBs), and laser

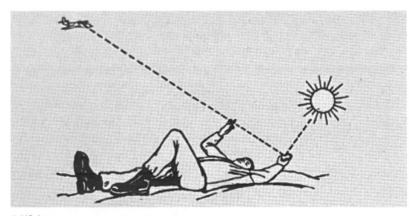

© US Army

markers, as well as many nonelectronic options such as signal fires, signal mirrors, signal panels, and smoke signals.

Communication is an essential element of the eight pillar survival concept and it can save your life or the lives of your loved ones in your most desperate hour. That said, being able to contact a rescue party and relay your position does not guarantee your survival, as you need to be able to keep yourself alive long enough for the rescue force to find and recover you.

While there is a plethora of communications devices available today, to simplify this pillar we are going to break it down into three categories: one-way comms, two-way comms, and signaling devices and techniques.

ONE-WAY COMMS
One-way communication devices offer the survivor the ability to monitor or send communication but not receive it. The following are examples of one-way comm devices:

SURVIVAL RADIO
One-way communication devices, also known as "passive" communication devices, such as survival radios offer the survivor the ability to monitor not only the formation or progress of a rescue party but also the threat of inclement

© Brian Morris

weather and other natural threats. It is smart to keep a survival radio in your EDC pack. What makes a radio a survival radio is that it has multiple ways to obtain power. Most survival radios have a solar panel, a rechargeable battery, a standard battery, and an emergency hand crank to produce power. Additionally, many survival radios possess a number of other functions like a USB port to charge your phone, a flashlight, and multiple other tools to aid in your survival and rescue.

PERSONAL LOCATOR BEACON (PLB)
PLBs are highly effective for self-recovery situations. It is important to understand that triggering your PLB send a signal to a satellite that will then transmit your signal to a national rescue and recovery asset that will result in a full-blown search and rescue operation. Triggering your PLB could come with a

© Brian Morris

huge tab if it is activated for any reason other than in a real world, life-and-death need for rescue.

TWO-WAY COMMS

Two-way communication devices allow the survivor to both send and receive messages in some manner, including voice and/or data. The following are considered two-way communication devices:

CELL PHONE

Most people will likely have a cell phone on their person when they find themselves in a survival scenario. During large scope emergencies, cell towers may go down or be too far out of range to make a voice call. If all you have is a cell phone and voice calling does not work, try text messaging since they work on totally different systems and frequencies. Texting typically works much longer than voice because text messages use comparatively little bandwidth. In any emergency, be sure to turn down your screen brightness, put your phone in battery save mode, and disable WI-FI to conserve battery life. The majority of smartphones have an internal GPS so make sure you know how to send a pin drop of your location to aid in your recovery. It can also help to use your smart phone to "share" your location with a friend or family member prior to venturing out into the wilderness.

> **Tip:** Smart phones run on batteries. Batteries drain and die without the ability to recharge. A great way to mitigate the chances of your smartphone dying in a survival scenario is to carry a charger with you. The best charger to have in a survival scenario is one that can use natural resources such as the sun or heat to create electricity to charge your device. You can also find hand crank chargers that are either standalone or part of another device such as an emergency radio.

SATELLITE PHONE

Satellite phones give the survivor the ability to contact people who may be able to help, but these phones depend on their ability to reach a satellite in the sky so their use may be limited by cloud coverage and other obstructions. They also require a battery to power them which can be an issue in a prolonged survival scenario.

SIGNALING DEVICES AND TECHNIQUES

Signals can be used as a "last mile" communications technique to help rescue parties zero in on your exact location or as a means of alerting or catching the attention of rescue teams or anyone who may be passing by the area that you are in. Even if you can communicate with rescuers, you still need to keep yourself alive until they get there. It takes time for rescuers to respond, especially in bad weather or when aircraft are needed. Whether you  need rescue or just some supplies, once rescuers or your buddies are in the area, you still need to get them to your precise location and that is when signaling devices will be most effective.

SURVIVAL SIGNAL MIRROR

Light from a glass signal mirror can be detected more than twenty miles away, so sweep the horizon with reflected light even if you cannot see any vehicles, boats, or aircraft. You can also apply retroreflective adhesive tape to the back of your signal mirror for night signaling. Retroreflective tape reflects light more effectively at night, greatly increasing visibility.

© US Army

SIGNAL PANEL

The signal panel is comprised of contrasting colors on opposite sides and can be folded to communicate prearranged messages. The military's VS-17 panel can be purchased online or from a military surplus store. You can make your own signal panel by purchasing a piece of highly visible material. You can add to its effectiveness by adding reflective materials to the panel.

© Brian Morris

> **Tip:** "Glide" tape can be purchased online and works extremely well as a visible reflective material that can even be seen at night by rescuers utilizing night vision goggles and infrared (IR) spotlights.

FLARE

Flares are a decent last mile signal that work day or night. Because they can be fired quickly, they are useful for signaling others that may not be in view long. Do not waste them if an aircraft is flying away from you.

© Brian Morris

FLASHLIGHT

A flashlight can make for an outstanding signaling tool. Many flashlights today have lumen strengths of well over 1000 which can be seen for miles and miles away.

© Brian Morris

FIREARMS

If you don't have a flare round or tracer round that can be seen, it is still possible that someone will hear your distress call if you fire your firearm in three consecutive shots. A succession of three shots is considered an international distress signal.

SMOKE (FIRE)

Place pine boughs and other live or wet wood products on top of hot fire(s) to create a white smoke plume. To increase the chances of your smoke being seen, try to keep a fire of hot embers constantly burning and consider building three like fires in a row (another international distress signal).

> **Caution:** Any time you are dealing with fire, you want to ensure that you take the appropriate steps to contain it so that it does not spread and potentially ignite a forest fire that could be hazardous or deadly and turn a bad situation even worse.

SMOKE (GRENADE)

It's a smart move to keep several smoke grenades in your EDC pack. You can get them online or in any fireworks store. Consider using grenades with unnatural colors such as florescent orange for the best chances of being seen.

STROBE

Strobe lights are effective for last mile signaling, but if you are signaling to an armed aircraft, use a blue filter so that your strobe will not be mistaken for gunfire. You can find strobe lights in most army surplus or outdoor adventure stores.

LASER

Signal lasers project a wide beam instead of a spot and can be used to signal many miles. You can rope or "corral" your position by moving the laser in a circular motion above your head to signal your exact location.

© Brian Morris

Caution: Do not point lasers directly at a rescue aircraft, as the laser light can be harmful or even blinding to the aircrew.

© Brian Morris

WHISTLE

Whistles work best in wilderness survival scenarios when you are trying to either be found or to vector in a search party to your exact location. Like other audible signal devices, use whistle blasts in successions of three to represent the international call for distress.

AIR HORN

An air horn is an excellent form of audio signaling, as it can be heard from great distances. You can find airhorns almost anyplace, from your local boating store to online. Like other audible signal devices, use horn blasts in successions of three to represent the international call for distress.

© Brian Morris

EMERGENCY SHAPE CODE SIGNALS

Number	Message	Code symbol
1	Require assistance.	V
2	Require medical assistance.	X
3	No or negative.	N
4	Yes or affirmative.	Y
5	Proceed in this direction.	↑

© US Army

Emergency Panel Signal:

© US Army

AIR TO GROUND SIGNALS/AIRCRAFT ACKNOWLEDGMENT SIGNALS

MESSAGE RECEIVED AND UNDERSTOOD

Aircraft will indicate that ground signals have been seen and understood by—

Day or moonlight: Rocking from side to side.

Night: Making green flashes with signal lamp.

MESSAGE RECEIVED BUT NOT UNDERSTOOD

Aircraft will indicate that ground signals have been seen but not understood by—

Day or night: Making a complete right hand circle.

Night: Making red flashes with signal lamp.

© US Army

INTERNATIONAL MORSE CODE

To signal SOS to a rescue party, all you need to do is make something on the ground that represents an unbroken sequence of three dots, three dashes, and three dots, with no spaces between the dots and dashes. You can write it in the sand, dig it in the snow, or use tree branches and other debris to write it in an open field. The important thing to remember is that it needs to be large enough to be easily recognizable from the air.

AIRCRAFT VECTORING PROCEDURES

If you can contact a friendly aircraft with a radio, guide the pilot to your location. Use the following general format to guide the pilot:

- Mayday, Mayday
- Call sign (if any)
- Name
- Location
- Number of survivors
- Available landing sites
- Any remarks such as medical aid or other specific types of help needed immediately

Note: Simply because you have made contact with rescuers does not mean that you are safe. Follow instructions and continue to use sound survival techniques until you are actually rescued.

Wilderness First Aid for the Nonmedical Professional

Disclaimer: The material in this chapter is written by wilderness medicine expert Mickey Fuentes, MD, and is for informational purposes only. It does not replace the counsel of a doctor or health-care professional.

© Brian Morris

The first rule of any survival situation is having the right attitude. If you find yourself in a situation where there are no first responders, nurses, or doctors, you must take care of yourself or your loved ones in the event of a medical emergency, serious illness, or injury. This chapter is broken down into four phases that can help you become a better wilderness medicine and first aid expert.

PHASE 1: PLAN

Having a good understanding of how to manage your health by learning the fundamentals of wilderness medicine and first aid are all important steps to self-preservation and overall preparedness for any survival situation that you may encounter. Progressive elaboration is a tool that can be used to help plan for any medical need by first starting with an idea and, as details or more information become available, adding to your plan. The key to planning is always having prevention and safety in mind when preparing for Wilderness, Austere, and Remote (W.A.R.) medicine:

- **W**ilderness medicine can range from taking a hike in a local park to participating in an expedition to Everest. For either occasion you must plan accordingly and ensure that you have the proper equipment such as an umbrella or poncho for rain, repellant for insects, sunscreen to protect you from the sun, or extreme cold weather and climbing gear if needed.

- **A**ustere medicine is when you find yourself unprepared for a survival or rescue situation, and have zero or limited resources available and must improvise with what you have. An example of this is being caught in a blizzard with a stalled car and no cell phone signal. In this case, you must evaluate your situation, make a list of available resources, and perform accordingly.

- **R**emote medicine is for those who choose to be off the grid or away in a rural area with limited access to nearby cities and towns. Since the response for rescue can be delayed, it is important to plan for any medical emergency and have the right tools to perform.

To begin planning, first write down the event you intend to participate in, such as a two-day hike in a national park. Next, make a list of necessary equipment such as specific clothing, special gear, and a medical kit for any medical problems and emergencies you may face. A good technique is to create a Primary, Alternate, Contingency, and Emergency (PACE) plan for your kit and include what external resources are available.

For the example of a two-day hike, a PACE plan would look like this:

Primary: Individual first aid kits for everyone participating in hike

Alternate: Large medical kit in vehicle in event of an emergency

Contingency: Seek assistance from park services and request medical kit on station

Emergency: Activate emergency response system (calling 9-1-1).

PHASE 2: PREPARE

To be prepared, a good understanding of the event in which you are participating will help in making decisions on which equipment to prioritize. Keep in mind that you can only use what you carry so having a trauma bag full of life saving equipment is neither practical, effective, nor efficient; you cannot carry everything. The general rule is to only carry necessary items and know how to effectively use them. If an item is large or bulky and serves one purpose, make sure that it is essential, or else find alternatives that are multipurpose and can serve other uses. Special Forces use the Massive Hemorrhage, Airway, Respiration, Circulation, Hypothermia (MARCH) algorithm to help set up equipment. However, keep in mind that this is designed for trauma and does not include medical emergencies. The following is an example of basic equipment to stock an aid bag or individual first aid kit.

Massive Hemorrhage
- Tourniquet
- Kerlix gauze
- Ace wrap
- Hemostatic packing agents
- Emergency trauma dressing
- Occlusive chest seals
- Abdominal dressing

Airway/Respiration
- Valved CPR face mask
- Nasal pharyngeal apparatus
- Oral pharyngeal apparatus
- Occlusive chest seals
- Bag Valve Mask (BVM)
- Laryngeal Mask Airway (LMA)
- CRIC kit
- 10G/14G/16G needle for decompression or cricothyroidotomy

Circulation
- IV kit
- Automated Electronic Defibrillator (AED)

Hypothermia
- Emergency survival blanket
- Ready heat blankets
- Pocket heaters

Other Medical Emergencies
- Over the counter (OTC) pain medication: ibuprofen, acetaminophen, naproxen
- Over the counter allergy medicine: diphenhydramine, loratadine (preferred for nondrowsy)
- Medical tape
- Medical shears
- Head lamp
- Tweezers
- Alcohol swabs
- Small adhesive bandages
- Splint material
- Triangular bandages
- Oral rehydration solution packet
- Flocculation tablets

PHASE 3: EXECUTE

All the planning and preparing in the world can never fully prepare you for a real-life emergency. It is your responsibility to understand what is happening to the patient and how every piece of equipment works in your kit (ensuring that you've checked expiration dates and batteries prior to your event) and do your best. There are three types of patients that we encounter in life: The first will die no matter what intervention we do, the second will live no matter the mistakes we make, and the third will live or die based on our actions; this is the patient we train for. In any situation, the first response should be to address life threatening injuries first, then remove the patient from the hazardous environment and begin treatment. The following are steps to take when a patient may be injured.

Step 1: Ensure that the scene is safe for you prior to getting to the patient and make sure you put on any available body substance isolations (BSI). The worst thing is to try and save somebody and find they were bitten by a snake or encountered a potent toxin and now you are a victim.

Step 2: Check for life threatening injuries! At this point, we are following the Massive Hemorrhage, Airway, Respiration, Circulation, Hypothermia (MARCH) algorithm. If severe bleeding is identified, apply direct pressure, and get a tourniquet on immediately. If there is any injury to the chest or abdomen, apply a chest seal, preferably a vented chest seal that allows for pleural chest pressure normalization.

> **Note:** It does not matter if the bleeding is arterial or venous; any severe bleeding can be life threatening so get it under control. Tourniquets should be applied high and tight regardless of how distal the wound Is. The goal is to stop all bleeding and later make corrections as necessary.

Step 3: Move the patient from any danger, hazards, or environmental threats that pose a risk. If a head injury is suspected, or if the patient fell from a height taller than their height or greater than a two-story building, suspect spinal cord injury and avoid moving until the C-spine (cervical spine/neck area) is properly controlled.

Step 4: Once a patient is safely removed and all life-threatening injuries are controlled, reassess any interventions that were made to ensure that they are still functioning properly. At this point, you can conduct a full primary patient survey, which includes the remainder of the MARCH algorithm. Most health-care professionals are familiar with the ABCDE of Primary surveys, which can be useful as well.

- Airway
- Breathing
- Circulation
- Disability
- Environmental/Exposure

PRIMARY SURVEY

Airway: Ensure that the patient has a clear airway by simply positioning the patient so that air has a way in and out. If the patient is unconscious or you suspect a neck injury, you can perform a head-tilt-chin-lift or jaw thrust to allow for air to move in and out. If alone or a more advanced airway is required, you can place a nasal pharyngeal apparatus (NPA) into the patient. The NPA can be tolerated by semiconscious patients; be cautious for a gag reflex. The NPA is measured from the edge of the right nostril to the lower lobe of the ear, and the diameter should be comparable to that of the patient's pinky finger. If the NPA is too long, use the trauma shears to cut it to size. Using a water-based lubricant (saliva can be used as a substitute; avoid using blood, as this can falsely indicate a head injury), insert the NPA with the bevel facing the septum, again watching for a gag reflex. If the patient is completely unconscious and the airway needs to be advanced, the oral pharyngeal apparatus (OPA) is a good choice. This is a rigid plastic device that holds the jaw open from within the mouth, allowing for air to flow in and out. The OPA is measured from the edge of the mouth to the angle of the jaw. An OPA kit comes in various sizes, so it is important to premeasure all team members and be prepared. The OPA cannot be modified and if it is too large it can activate a gag reflex, causing vomiting and leading to aspiration, or if it is too short it can push the tongue back and cause an obstruction. The most advanced airways that are reserved for health-care providers include inserting a tube directly down the patient's throat, known as a laryngeal mask airway (LMA), or creating a direct channel through the cricothyroid either through a needle or surgical cut. Based on the skill level, these procedures are better reserved for trained personnel.

Breathing: Children, choking, and drowning patients require two rescue breaths prior to initiating CPR or going through the primary survey when pulseless. Breathing can be accomplished by direct mouth-to-mouth contact; this is usually avoided due to risk of exposure to and/or infection caused by unknown pathogens or toxins. CPR valve masks are available that offer a barrier when performing rescue breaths. The bag valve mask (BVM) is the ideal choice, as this allows for good airflow and compliant chest rise and fall.

Circulation: While conducting a primary survey, obtaining vitals is a crucial part in identifying if treatment is effective. A pulse check using the carotid pulse is a good way to tell if the unconscious patient is suffering from a cardiac-related episode. During the planning phase, it is important to identify any team members with preexisting conditions and plan accordingly. If a carotid pulse is not felt after ten seconds of checking, the emergency response system should be activated, and the patient should be handed over to higher levels of care. While waiting for rescuers, CPR can be initiated to maintain proper circulation and increase chances of survival. It is recommended that all team members attend a CPR certification course to familiarize themselves with the proper protocol.

Disability: This refers to any bone or joint injury that inhibits the patient from removing themselves from danger and getting to the proper care. Dislocations can be reduced in the field with proper training; the goal is to seek treatment immediately to assess for any other life-threatening conditions. Fractures run the risk of losing limb and life and should be treated urgently. They can be closed with no bone exposure or open with bone protruding through the skin. Manipulation can cause vessel rupture and make the situation worse and should only be attempted if emergency response services are delayed due to environment or location and pulses are not obtainable. Splinting should be done to isolate the joint above and below the injury. It would be necessary to assist the patient to safety, and proper planning can identify clear routes that offer less obstacles and safer transport.

Environmental/Exposure: The elements can be a great cause for injury. If the cause is extreme cold weather, the risk of frostbite is high and rewarming should be limited only if the patient is not at risk of reexposure. Cold weather can reduce cardiac activity as well as clotting ability (we discuss the lethal triad on page 130). In addition, you have environmental threats such as dangerous fauna and poisonous or toxic plants.

- Poison ivy

- Poison oak

• Poison sumac

POISON SUMAC

In a survival situation, water is one of the most crucial resources that can be challenging to procure. In addition to finding or maintaining a good source of clean water and a regular supply of food, good field sanitation, and hygiene are important tasks, and if unattended can lead to rapid spread of disease and illness. Keeping clean and sanitary will mitigate the risk of spreading infectious diseases and prevent illness. It is essential to keep your area clean and sanitary to avoid disease and avoid attracting unwanted animals, and to have an in-depth knowledge of first aid, CPR, and wilderness medicine.

MEDICAL EMERGENCIES

When planning an excursion, we tend to focus on preparing for traumatic injuries or events and avoid planning or preparing for medical emergencies. Medical emergencies can turn a fun trip into a nightmare and even into a complete catastrophe. If a patient presents with a life-threatening emergency, immediately begin the MARCH algorithm and, once stabilized, continue with the primary survey. If the patient continues to deteriorate or the situation is beyond your capabilities and training, immediately activate the emergency response system from your PACE plan. A more detailed secondary survey can be completed for a patient that presents with non-life-threatening injuries, or the cause of illness is unknown. One technique is to create a Subjective, Objective, Assessment, Plan (SOAP) note. The first part of any survey is to collect baseline vitals and annotate any intervention.

Subjective: The subjective part of the SOAP note is to collect as much information from the patient. One helpful tool is to go through the exam the same way every time. Start with the vitals, and the chief complaint, then collect as much information as possible.

Objective: Once you complete the subjective part, you can start reviewing and examining the patient. Remember to always go from least invasive to more invasive. Never remove clothing in extreme temperatures if there is a risk of reexposure and always request permission before touching the patient. **Tip:** Always talk to your patient as you work your way through each survey; this comforts your patient and lets them know what to expect, giving them a sense of security.

Assessment: With all the information you have collected, it is time to make a list of what you think is going on. This can be beneficial when handing over the patient to higher levels of care by reducing the amount of time the provider would have to go through to collect the information you have already obtained. The best practice is to make your list according to the worst diagnosis to the least worrisome.

Plan: You made it this far, and now it is time to decide. Do you continue with your trip or excursion, or do you activate the emergency response service and get the patient to a higher level of care?

Tip: A low energy state due to lack of water and food can cause an altered mental status and should not be taken lightly. Staying hydrated and eating regularly can help minimize effects of dehydration and hypoglycemia. Other conditions that can cause an altered mental status include drugs and toxins, heat exhaustion, and heat stroke. If available, a glucometer is recommended to rule out life-threatening hypoglycemia. Collecting a good history is crucial to identify the insulting factor. Nausea, vomiting, and diarrhea are three of the worst symptoms to have in any situation, even more so when you are far from the comfort of home and away from indoor plumbing. Three of the worst culprits that can be life threatening are cholera, giardia, and hepatitis A; all three are related to drinking or eating contaminated food and water, showing how important it is to maintain a clean supply of drinking water and to properly prepare your food intake.

SPECIAL CONSIDERATIONS

High altitude: At elevations greater than 2,500 meters above sea level, most people begin to experience symptoms related to lack of oxygen or hypoxia due to the hypobaric environment. The typical presentation is often called acute mountain sickness (AMS) and can be experienced by rapid ascent to higher elevation. This can even be experienced by personnel airlifted by helicopters to higher elevations. Common symptoms are headaches, nausea, and/or vomiting. The treatment is simple: discontinue the ascent and rest or descend and rest. For more severe cases of AMS, acetazolamide can be used in conjunction with descend and rest. More severe complications of high altitude include high-altitude cerebral edema and high-altitude pulmonary edema. High-altitude cerebral edema presents like AMS, but the symptoms can be more severe with notable changes in level of consciousness and altered mental status. The treatment calls for immediate descent and in addition to acetazolamide, dexamethasone should be given. High-altitude pulmonary edema is also a life-threatening emergency and calls for immediate descent with the administration of acetazolamide and nifedipine which can help reduce pulmonary arterial pressure and the pulmonary edema. In all cases of altitude sickness, the decision should allow for descent and additional treatment if needed. AMS does not necessitate evacuation, but high-altitude cerebral edema and high-altitude pulmonary edema are life-threatening emergencies and warrant an evacuation and evaluation by higher levels of care.

Diving: Almost the opposite of high altitude is diving and increased pressure. When a diver enters the water and begins to descend, every ten meters roughly one atmosphere of pressure is added on the body. This pressure can be the cause of injury or illness and is often referred to as dysbarism. Signs and symptoms can range from minor things like earaches and sinus pain to major things like gas toxicity, gas embolism, and decompression sickness. Treatment includes controlled ascent to avoid barotrauma, and possibly hyperbaric therapy. It is recommended when participating is such high-risk activities to do so in the presence of trained and skilled professionals. Diving into open water already poses high risk but there are additional elements to consider such as wildlife like sharks, barracuda, and other large curious sea creatures; not to mention the venomous ones like the blue ringed octopus and box jellyfish. A frightened diver doing a rapid ascent can cause severe injuries such as barotrauma to the ears and sinuses as well as barotrauma to the lungs. In addition, divers and anyone participating in recreational water sports run the risk of drowning. The first ten meters of a dive or submersion are the most challenging for the body because of the drastic changes from one atmosphere to two. Shallow water blackout is a dangerous consequence of such changes and can occur to even seasoned divers, increasing the risk of drowning. The management of a near-drowning victim is to immediately and safely remove them from the water and give them two rescue breaths. A common complication of near-drowning is cardiopulmonary arrest, at which time evacuation is necessary, as well as initiating CPR. If available, an automated electronic defibrillator (AED) should be placed on the patient and the emergency medical system should be activated.

Lightning: Although lightning strikes are not that common, they occur more often than expected. The typical timing for a lightning strike is just before and after a storm and usually in the afternoon. This is good information to know because it can help you prepare by avoiding activities during these times if a storm is approaching. Lightning strikes can be direct or indirect and can affect single or multiple people at once. Direct strikes are the most dangerous. Although they pass through the body rapidly, they tend to inflict the most damage due to changes in resistance throughout the body that cause effects like shorts in a circuit. You do not necessarily have to be directly hit by lightning to fall victim. If you are in close proximity to a lightning strike, the energy can arch away and strike you. It will also travel through the ground again, using the human body as a conduit due to resistance changes. A common complication is damage to the eyes and ears, causing blindness and/or deafness. Severe consequences of a direct lightning strike include cardiopulmonary arrest, at which point evacuation is mandatory and CPR should be initiated. A lot of the effects of a lightning strike can be delayed due to the rapid discharge of energy inside the body, so it is recommended that any person struck by lightning regardless of presentation should seek medical assistance from higher levels of care.

Burns: Burns are a major cause of concern due to their inherent risk of infection. Depending on the severity of the burn, avoid activities that increase the risk of burn or heat exhaustion. In addition, if the environment is cold, heaters and stoves pose a greater risk for accidental burns and possibly carbon monoxide poisoning. Campfires should be controlled and contained, and campers should avoid sleeping close to them to avoid the risk of sleeping bags catching fire, as nylon and other materials melt into a liquid form that can cause severe burns. Treat all burns by removing the source and attempting to keep them wet and warm. Avoid applying cold packing, as this will force the heat to go deeper into the tissues. A patient with circumferential burns regardless of location should be evacuated to higher levels of care.

Bites and stings: People react differently to bites and stings from insects, but there are a few insects that we should all avoid. As we have learned from both the MARCH algorithm and the primary survey, airways are important. Things that we want to watch out for when someone is bitten are signs of swelling and spread and difficulty breathing. Shortness of breath can be a sign of worse things to come. If the patient has excess saliva, this can be an early indicator of swelling in the throat and an emergency. Anaphylaxis is our main concern when it comes to insect bites and stings. If a patient has been exposed to a trigger, we remove the patient from that trigger and begin our assessment. If the patient has a known allergy to the trigger, it is best to check if the patient has a prescribed autoinjector of epinephrine and assist them in administrating it to themselves. If they are unaware of an allergy to the trigger and are experiencing shortness of breath or difficulty breathing, you can administer diphenhydramine or loratadine based on your situation. Although diphenhydramine is a better-acting agent, a side effect is drowsiness which, if a long trek back to an evacuation point is necessary, can become extremely difficult with a nonambulatory patient.

Dental: This subject is less covered in most books due to its complexity, but it is important to understand that the majority of the incidents that happen in the wilderness are dental related and can have a major impact on the life of an individual if not managed properly. Our mouths are not necessarily the cleanest parts of our bodies, and infections can spread rapidly, creating havoc. A tooth fracture can make it difficult if not impossible to consume foods, and abscesses can fester and lead to complication and even death. Proper prevention is important, including regular cleaning and taking care with good oral hygiene to avoid issues in the future. For short excursions or activities a numbing gel can minimize the pain and help until the patient can be seen by a dentist, but in longer-term scenarios it is best to evacuate or transport to higher levels of care.

Shock: Shock is the inability to get oxygen to the organs of your body. The lethal triad is a list of problems that feed into each other, making it harder to keep the patient from going into shock and eventually dying. The first point of the lethal triad is coagulopathy, which is a fancy way of saying that the body has no way to stop its own bleeding. Blood is an essential part of our bodies and physiologically it helps us stay alive by performing many tasks. If you have a major bleed, one important task of blood is to form a clot, which it accomplishes using platelets. The reason we always start our assessments with MARCH is because your patient is more likely to die from a major bleed than any of the other injuries. The more blood we lose, the fewer platelets we have and the more we bleed.

The second part of the lethal triad is hypothermia. Another crucial task of blood is to regulate and maintain our temperature. We must maintain active heat for our metabolism which can help with the clotting factors. Losing blood not only reduces the number of platelets but also lowers the body's core temperature.

The third part of the lethal triad is acidosis. This is by far the most complex and I will do my best to explain this. Our body requires simple necessities to stay alive, including water, food, and oxygen. As we take in food, we convert it into energy for our body and release waste products, and the same holds true for water. It gets a little more complex with oxygen. We use oxygen as we breathe it in and convert it into energy for our cells, but in cases of extreme stress our bodies can make energy without using oxygen with some consequences. For example, if you go to the gym and do a hard workout, this represents extreme stress. As you work out, your body goes from an aerobic state (using oxygen) to an anerobic state (no oxygen). The consequences can be felt the next day when you wake up with sore muscles because of the lactic acid that built up in your body. We can live through a workout, but imagine this taking place in every part of your body and you have no control. That is what happens during shock. Too much acid in our blood is bad because it can cause irreversible damage to organs in our bodies and break down platelets that keep us from bleeding out.

We have just discussed hemorrhagic or hypovolemic shock, but there are various other forms including neurogenic shock, septic shock, anaphylactic shock, and cardiogenic shock. It is necessary to prevent and treat shock in all injured personnel. If the patient is conscious, place them on a level surface with the lower extremities elevated to help blood flow to the brain. If the victim is unconscious, place them on their side or abdomen with their head turned to one side to prevent choking on vomit, blood, or other fluids; this is known as the left lateral recumbent position.

PHASE 4: REASSESS

All the hard work and dedication, all the effort given to save a life mean nothing if you do not reassess your patient. Every intervention that you perform has the risk of failing, and every movement you conduct has the potential to worsen any condition. You must treat your patient as a critical patient and reassess them as often as possible. The general rule is to reevaluate any intervention and obtain a new set of vitals every five minutes based on the presentation of the patient. If the patient is unconscious, check them more often.

All patients that are deemed critical enough for transport should be handed over to a provider of equal or greater care. Once you have a good understanding of your available resources, you can plan, prepare, and execute accordingly.

EVACUATION GUIDELINES

Scene safety is a priority. Most accidents or injuries take place in areas with difficult access or that pose an immediate threat to others. These areas are designated as red zones. You can utilize stopgaps such as direct pressure or tourniquets on massive hemorrhages, but you eventually need to relocate this patient to an area that is safer. The area you move to might not be ideal but should afford you the opportunity to identify any issues you may have missed while in the red zone, so you always want to reassess your patient as often as you can. This new area is designated as a yellow zone if the threat is not as high as before but you are not completely out of risk. Once a patient is secure and handed over to higher levels of care or they can continue without the risk of further injury or illness, you are in the green zone.

The three zones are concepts that help us determine the appropriate treatment measure and when to use them. For example, it would not be appropriate to conduct a secondary survey on a patient who slipped down a boulder and had their leg trapped in a boulder with a large laceration. In this case, you would go through M of MARCH and, once bleeding is controlled, attempt to free them and relocate them to a safer area to conduct a primary survey to identify any other issues or injuries. If you are responsible for multiple patients at once, you can centralize them into a casualty collection point to maximize your treatment efforts.

Let's put it all together! As an example, let's say you are planning a hike to a national park with trails that follow the base of a mountain. You begin your planning phase by determining what clothing, tools, and equipment you will need to have fun on your trip. You acquire maps and plan your route and determine it will be a four-day outing.

As part of medical planning, you check online and collect information pertaining to the emergency response system and find that there are park rangers trained as paramedics with a medical shed that can provide excellent prehospital care similar to an urgent care, there is an air-rescue unit that has the capability to rescue on near vertical platforms and within deep foliage, and finally there are major roads approximately eight miles from the hiking trails where ambulance services can transport patients to the nearest trauma center. In addition to your available resources, you want to research the wildlife and natural fauna found in the area you will be hiking. You want to identify any animals that might be a threat like bears and cougars, as well as poisonous plants and animals common to the area. You can look at historical data to get an idea of the typical weather patterns for the time of year you will be conducting your trip and regularly check with the weather station for changes.

For preparation, you want to include items that you know will be beneficial in the event of injury. Bleeding from an injury is a real threat and tourniquets should be one of the first items you pack. Try to create a list of potential threats, injuries, and illnesses and the items needed to treat them and make a first aid pack. You cannot carry everything so plan and prepare accordingly.

The day has finally arrived, and you are off to your trip with three other good friends. You hiked all day and are exhausted from all the hard work. As you and your friend prepare the campsite, you take charge and instruct everyone to please maintain a clean site, especially not to leave food out that can attract unwanted visitors. You also mention that any "nature calls" should be at least two hundred feet away and to please let everyone know when you are leaving and when you come back. Everyone gets ready for bed, and no one is sleeping too close to the fire.

The next day, you begin your hike to the next campsite, and one of your friends begins complaining about a headache. Stop in a rest area and begin a secondary survey. You conduct a head-to-toe assessment and find no significant findings. You determine that the mountain range is well below 2,500 meters above sea level, and your friend claims they did not sleep near the campfire. You tell them to drink more water and will reassess them at the next rest stop. When you reached your second campsite, your friend has greatly improved. The added regimes of water has made their headache go away, and they feel better. Same as the night before, campsite operations continue.

The next morning, you begin your hike to the third and final campsite when the same friend from yesterday accidently stumbles while trying to jump over a downed log. They stopped their fall with an outstretched hand and sustain a nasty cut along their forearm from a nearby branch. As you witness this, you also note that the downed log is home to a hornet's nest and your friend has now sustained multiple bites. The first thing you do is cover yourself and go to your friend and apply direct pressure to the wound and assist them away from that location. You reach into your first aid kit and pull out a tourniquet, as the bleeding is severe, and your friend is screaming from both the pain and the sight of extreme bleeding. After placing the tourniquet high and tight until the bleeding stops, you immediately start assessing your friend by continuing with the MARCH algorithm. Bleeding is controlled and airway, respiration, and circulation are good; your friend did not sustain any head injuries. A few moments pass and your friend begins to complain about difficulty breathing and could possibly be having a reaction to the hornet stings. You immediately check your med plan and decide that the best option is to walk your friend to the nearest clearing that is two hours away and air them to the nearest hospital. In the meantime, you collect a good set of vitals and administer loratadine to your friend to avoid drowsiness so that they can reduce time by walking themselves to the clearing. The loratadine has minimized the effect of the hornet stings, and your friend is starting to feel a little bit better. However, based on the likely chances that if this were true anaphylaxis, the risk of complete airway closure is great, they must be handed off to the next higher level of care.

Prior to handing off your friend to air rescue, you want to reassess the tourniquet. You hand off all information obtained from your surveys along with a list of interventions and collect information on where they will be transported. You and the other friends trek back to your vehicles and head to the hospital to meet up with your friend.

Hopefully, this was helpful in clarifying the steps and methods for proper planning, preparing, executing, and reassessing for wilderness medicine. There is no one right way of providing care, but these tools are always available for you if the need arises.

DANGEROUS INSECTS AND ARACHNIDS

It is very important in a survival situation to know what insects to steer clear of or at least to understand which ones have the ability to do you harm. This is particularly important if you or a member of your group has any predisposed allergies to insect stings or if you are presenting signs of an allergic  reaction to a sting. If you are stung and showing signs of a severe reaction and not able to get medical attention or to receive a shot of epinephrine, it is imperative that you try to remain calm.

- Flies
  - Spread disease
  - Horseflies have a painful bite
- Mosquitoes
  - Spread disease
  - Menacing sting
- Scorpions
  - Painful sting
  - Venomous
  - Live on every continent accept Antarctica

Tip: You can cook and eat a scorpion whole since direct sustained heat negates the harmful effects of their venom.

- Brown recluse spider
  - Brown with a dark brown or black violin shape on the back of its head
  - Found only in the South and Central United States
  - Necrotic venom
  - Severe reactions could cause a large, volcano-like lesion with the damaged tissue becoming gangrenous

- Funnel-web spider (native to Australia)
  - Highly toxic bite
  - Nausea, vomiting, high blood pressure, unconsciousness, and sometimes death may occur

- Tarantula
  - Bite similar to a bee sting unless an allergic reaction occurs

- Black widow
  - All black with a red hourglass shape on its back
  - Severe burning, swelling, and pain at bite site
  - May see two fang marks at bite site
  - Venom affects the nervous system

- Centipede
  - Venomous bite
  - Painful but rarely fatal to humans unless an allergic reaction is experienced
- Bees, wasps, and hornets
  - Unlike a bee that can sting only once, a wasp can sting multiple times
  - Sharp pain, burning, and swelling at the sting site
  - Large, red welt; painful
  - Can cause anaphylaxis

Bee   Wasp   Hornet

Tip: In the absence of medication, you can put a thin layer of mud over a sting site. The coolness of the mud will help ease the pain and it is said that as the mud dries it will help draw the toxins caused by the sting from the body.

- Ticks
  - Can spread Lyme disease and other diseases
  - Try to remove with head intact
  - Adverse reactions include larger sized lesions, inflamed areas, and a menacing itch

- Red bugs (chiggers)
  - Adverse reactions include larger sized lesions, inflamed areas, and a menacing itch
  - Like to bite at folds of skin or where clothing and skin meet such as at the belt area

- Red ant
  - Painful bite
  - Menacingly painful, small, blister-like reaction is common

Tip: If you can manage to kill a bunch of red ants without getting all bitten up, crush them up and make a paste out of them. You can use it like a spice to add to meat in order to get rid of its gamy flavor.

Tip: Always try to kill whatever bites/stings you so that you or medical personnel can identify the creature and better care for the bite/sting.

Tip: Studies suggest that stinging nettle can effectively treat a wide range of health concerns including insect bites.

ALLERGIC REACTIONS TO BITES

According to the Mayo Clinic, life-threatening allergic reaction (anaphylaxis) can cause shock, a sudden drop in blood pressure, and trouble breathing. In people who have an allergy, anaphylaxis can occur minutes after exposure to a specific allergy-causing substance (allergen). In some cases, there may be a delayed reaction or anaphylaxis may occur without an apparent trigger.

In a survival situation where advanced medical aid is unavailable, if you or one of the people you are with is having an allergic reaction with signs of anaphylaxis, follow the protocol below and try to help them remain as calm as possible by taking slow and controlled breaths.

- Ask the person if they are carrying an epinephrine autoinjector (EpiPen, Auvi-Q, etc.) to treat an allergy attack.
- If the person says he or she needs to use an autoinjector, ask

whether you should help inject the medication. This is usually done by pressing the autoinjector against the person's thigh.

- Have the person lie still on their back.
- Loosen tight clothing and cover the person with a blanket. Don't give the person anything to drink.
- If there's vomiting or bleeding from the mouth, turn the person on their side to prevent choking.
- If there are no signs of breathing, coughing, or movement, begin CPR. Do uninterrupted chest presses—about one hundred every minute—until paramedics arrive (if you are in a situation where 911 is available).
- Get emergency treatment even if symptoms start to improve. After anaphylaxis, it's possible for symptoms to recur. Monitoring in a hospital for several hours is usually necessary.

Signs and symptoms of anaphylaxis include:
- Skin reactions, including hives, itching, and flushed or pale skin
- Swelling of the face, eyes, lips, or throat
- Constriction of the airways leading to wheezing and trouble breathing
- A weak and rapid pulse
- Nausea, vomiting, or diarrhea
- Dizziness, fainting, or unconsciousness

Some common anaphylaxis triggers include:
- Medications
- Foods such as peanuts, tree nuts, fish, and shellfish
- Insect stings from bees, yellow jackets, wasps, hornets, and fire ants

If you've had any kind of severe allergic reaction in the past, ask your doctor if you should be prescribed an epinephrine autoinjector to carry with you.

> **Caution:** An adverse reaction to any bite or sting can be deadly, so as a precaution, immediate medical attention should be sought whenever possible.

ABOUT MICKEY FUENTES, MD

Dr. Mickey Fuentes served with the US Army for eleven years, with most of that time assigned to the 7th Special Force Group (Airborne) as an 18E Special Forces Communications Sergeant, then as an 18D Special Forces

Medical Sergeant. He was honorably discharged as a Sergeant First Class after multiple combat deployments to Afghanistan in support of Operation Enduring Freedom. After his time in the military, Mickey created programs of instruction in flight, survival, and tactical medicine. He focused on wilderness, austere, remote, and prolonged field care medicine and currently teaches this through his and his wife's company, Native Element Medical in Miami, Florida. He completed a BS degree in strategic studies and defense analysis as well as an MBA with a concentration in project management at Norwich University in Vermont. Dr. Fuentes holds a doctor of medicine degree from the Medical University of Silesia in Poland. He is currently working on a PhD in public health with a focus on health promotion and disease prevention. Additionally, Dr. Fuentes is an active member of the Wilderness Medical Society.

Land Navigation

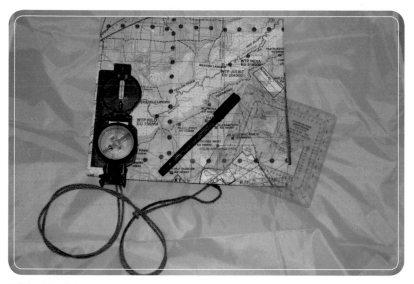

© Brian Morris

L et's admit that not everyone has the most solid land navigation skills and in fact there is a large group of outdoorsmen who would be in a large amount of trouble if the batteries on their GPS were to die midway through their outdoor excursion. One of the biggest dangers associated with hunters getting lost in the wilderness is panic. You should never let fear overtake your ability to make rational decisions. Finding your way out of the wilderness after becoming disoriented will require you to stay calm and use your knowledge of land navigation to get back on track. If you plan to spend time in the wilderness, you should at least attempt to learn navigation skills or at a very minimum have a plan for what to do when and if you or any member of your party gets lost.

People who have land navigation skills never get lost; they only get disoriented. When a person is lost, they do not have the skills to use the terrain, stars, nature, or their equipment to aid them in reorienting themselves and finding their way back to wherever it is they came from. On the other hand, when a person is disoriented, they may not know where they are, but they will have the confidence and training to utilize the terrain as well as nature, stars, their gear, and even math to reorient themselves quickly and get back on track.

Small children just learning to enjoy the outdoors may not have the best navigational skills, so they need to understand what to do if they get separated from their party. Since learning does not happen overnight and most people are not going to stop going into the wilderness cold turkey until their navigational skills are up to par, it is imperative that everyone in your group knows what to do in the event that they become separated or find themselves disoriented or lost.

One of the many acronyms that Green Berets have drilled into their heads is the acronym SLLS (pronounced "Sills"), which stands for **Stop, Look, Listen, and Smell**. The first thing a person should do when they find themselves lost or disoriented is to stop and try to make as little noise as possible so that they can take in their natural environment and so that noises like people calling their name, whistles, vehicles, streams, and busy roads will all be amplified. After conducting SLLS, it will be time to make a decision: stay in place and wait for someone to find you or begin to walk and find your own way out.

Another great acronym that you can use to help you decide if you should move or stay in place is called HITMET, which stands for **Health, Illumination, Training, Materials, Elements, and Terrain**. Health is very important because if you are sick, injured, or out of shape, that will factor into your decision to move or stay in place. Illumination is important because if it is about to get dark, you may want to consider other needs that will soon be more important than finding your way out such as food, water, and shelter. Your training in both land navigation skills and wilderness survival will play a huge role in your choice of action; the fewer skills you have, the better idea it is to stay in one location and wait for rescue. Materials refer to the equipment you have with you and the natural resources available to you for navigation and survival. Firearms, flairs, whistles, and air horns are all good ways to let people know your location. Maps, compasses, protractors, and GPSs are all good materials to help you reorient yourself. The elements can be a gigantic factor in the decision-making process. There may be times where shelter and warmth take precedence over all other needs due to a sudden change in the weather. Finally, you need to take terrain into consideration. Are you in the mountains where you can use terrain association or a map to help you find your way? Is there a water source to help you survive? What about a river or stream that you can follow back to civilization? Rivers and other prominent terrain features can help you locate your position on the ground and guide you to safety.

Remember, the best way to eliminate fear and panic from the equation is through education. The more you know the less you will panic and the easier it will be for you to reorient yourself and find your way. Land navigation is an often-neglected pillar of survival. If you cannot effectively navigate, you cannot operate or effect self-recovery, becoming dependent on others to come rescue you. Survivors should stay with vehicles or aircraft in noncombat situations and only move if necessary.

WHEN TO MOVE

Area lacks critical resources: Once you have hunted and foraged an area out, you need to move on to an area with more resources. If an area does not have adequate water or shelter, staying put can equate to death.

Area is unsafe: Security should always take priority in any survival situation. If you are aware of threats that make the area unsafe, move on to another location.

You are certain of your location: If you know where you are, where you need to be, and can reasonably get there, self-recovery may be more effective than rescue.

> **Note:** If you are in a survival ordeal and do need to move, leave a note in a plastic bag and trail signs indicating your planned direction of travel. The note should detail planned route of travel, destination, condition, and supplies. If your vehicle is found, they will also find your note. Construct a signal at the site so rescuers have reason to believe that you survived.

ELECTRONICS

A GPS, laser range finder, and other electronic gadgets are all excellent and highly efficient navigational tools, but do not bet your life on anything that

runs on batteries. Remember to apply PACE to all of your navigational tools and be sure that at least the emergency plan does not require batteries.

MAGNETIC COMPASSES

The two pieces of equipment that are most crucial to land navigation are the map and compass. The compass is the more critical of the two.

BUTTON COMPASS

A button compass is a small compass that is about the size of a button and is designed to be carried in your personal survival kit in your EDC bag.

LENSATIC COMPASS

The lensatic compass is a precision tool. Military surplus lensatic compasses are illuminated with tritium so that they can be seen in the dark without having to constantly be recharged with a flashlight. Just like it is nice to have a knife you can depend on, a quality compass is well worth what you will spend on it. Lensatic compasses have features that enable them to correct for magnetic declination and take precise bearings which are then sighted through folding "sights." This is helpful to pick out distant landmarks very precisely. The lensatic compass also makes it very easy to orient maps. Even the right map will not do much good until you get it pointed in the right direction.

TOPOGRAPHIC MAPS

Topographic maps are maps with 3D information about terrain features in the form of contour lines. Contour lines mark the altitude of terrain. If the lines are spaced close together, that means you are looking at a cliff. If they are spaced very far apart, that represents a flat area on the map. Military topographical maps we use on foot are in the scale of 1:25,000. The United States Geological Survey (USGS) topographical maps come in a variety of scales, but the most useful for foot travel are in the scale of 1:24,000 which is very close to the scale of military maps. The USGS website is full of great information detailing the symbols used on their maps. Use the information contained in map legends. Map legends often indicate symbols used, scale,

© Brian Morris

and magnetic declination, which is the difference between grid north and magnetic north in the area represented by the map.

PROTRACTOR

The Improved Military Style UTM/MGRS Coordinate Scale protractor has the most useful tools for orienteering combined into one protractor. It is helpful to transfer coordinates from the Military Grid Reference System, that the military uses, to the Universal Transvers Mercator coordinate system used by GPS manufacturers and vice versa.

PACE BEADS AND PACE COUNT

Pace counting is used to track distance traveled in paces or kilometers. Pace counting is important for estimating distance traveled, especially at night. The military uses a tool for pace counting called pace beads (aka "ranger beads"). You can purchase a set of pace beads or you can easily improvise them from a strand of paracord and beads or by using knots in place of beads. Pace beads are generally separated into two sets (a set of nine beads on the bottom and a set of five beads on

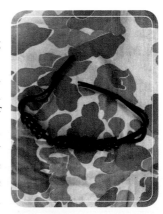

© Brian Morris

the top) and are slid downward to hold a count. To use pace beads, you first need to know what your personal pace count is.

How to get your personal pace count:
Start by first seeing how many paces of a single foot (as in, count every time your left foot hits the ground) it takes to walk a known distance of one hundred meters.

Once you have walked and calculated your pace three consecutive times, add all three pace counts together and divide by three. Whatever that number is will be your personal pace count.

Example:
Pace Attempt 1: 76
Pace Attempt 2: 74
Pace Attempt 3: 73
76 + 74 + 73 = 223
223 divided by 3 = 74
Your Pace Count = **74**

To use your pace beads, every time you reach your pace count of seventy-four, slide one row of nine pace beads down to represent one hundred meters walked. The top column of beads represents one thousand meters (or one kilometer) and you can slide down a bead each time you have slid all nine beads down and have come to the one hundred meter mark ten consecutive times.

The other aspect of pace counting to consider is that it is affected by terrain, so you must adjust your pace count for the type of terrain you travel. Your stride will lengthen traveling downhill and shorten traveling uphill. Wind affects pace, too. A tailwind will lengthen pace and a headwind will shorten it. Snow, ice, and even different clothing and shoes affect pace, so it is important that you actually measure your pace instead of estimating. Green Berets are masters of land navigation and orienteering and must be able to navigate great distances while carrying equipment exceeding 120 pounds and do so under the most extreme and austere of conditions.

> **Tip:** If you're in a pinch and you don't have a set of pace beads to measure how far you have traveled, you can pick up ten pebbles, twigs, or any small disposable object and drop one every time you reach your one hundred meter mark.

LANDMARKS

Any time you set out, whether it is from a hotel in a new city, a hole-up site or camp, take a look around. Get your bearings and notice where the mountains are, the rivers, coastline, and other prominent features. Take a look at your compass and find north. Now, look around. Which direction is uphill/downhill? If you are traveling in a car and especially if you are staring at a GPS or a map, you may remember everything as being flat, but it isn't, it is? Now, look at tall buildings and hills and mountains. Man-made structures can be great landmarks, too. Pick features you can recognize a long way off. These are landmarks. Notice any rivers and surface water in the area. What direction does the water flow? These are very important things to understand. Observe the shape of the drainage area. Many instructors will tell you to follow the rivers because they always flow to the sea. It is a good rule of thumb but is not always true. In the Great Basin of the USA, the rivers do not flow to the sea, and the Great Basin is a huge area. Look at the drainage of the area and major rivers because they are key landmarks, transportation routes, and a source of water, which brings us to lines of drift.

LINES OF DRIFT

Lines of drift are basically the lines of least resistance upon which people and animals tend to walk.

- Roads
- Riverbanks
- Ridges
- Fence lines
- Animal or hiking trails
- Power lines
- Train tracks

Lines of drift are extremely important for helping the survivor in finding their way.

FIELD-EXPEDIENT DIRECTION FINDING

While the magnetic compass is the most convenient way to navigate, it is certainly not the only way. Folks had been navigating for tens of thousands of years before compasses came into being.

LUNAR NAVIGATION

Whenever you have a crescent moon, you have a tool to find south. Just draw a line bisecting the two points of the crescent moon down to the horizon to find south.

LUNAR COMPASS

Drive a stake into the ground on any moonlit night and mark the tip of the shadow with a rock. Do it again after ten minutes or so. Draw a line between the two stones and that line will run east to west. The first rock will be to the west.

SOLAR NAVIGATION

Solar navigation is much like the lunar method. Pound a yard-long stick upright into level ground. Mark the tip of the shadow with a rock. Wait twenty minutes and mark it again. Draw a straight line through the rocks. The line will run east to west and the first rock will be to the west. This method works in both hemispheres. If you keep this going all day, the shortest shadow will indicate north-south. The north-south line will always run perpendicular to the east-west line.

1 Mark the shadow's tip.

2 Mark the new position and draw a line through the two marks.

3 Stand with the first mark to your left and the second mark to your right—you are now facing north.

© US Army

FLOATING NEEDLE COMPASS

Magnetize a thin sewing needle by stroking it with a piece of silk (or through your hair) in one direction from point to eye, just like the air passes over an arrow as it flies through the air. In the northern hemisphere, the needle will point north when floated in a leaf. You can buy maps printed on silk just like the old E&E maps and blood chits that used to be sewn into flight jackets. Alternatively, you can magnetize the needle by winding an insulated wiring around it and passing current through the wire for a few minutes.

© Survivapedia

NAVIGATION USING STARS

THE NORTHERN SKY

The main constellations to learn are the Ursa Major, also known as the Big Dipper or the Plow, and Cassiopeia. Neither of these constellations ever sets. They are always visible on a clear night. Use them to locate Polaris, also known as the polestar or the North Star. The North Star forms part of the Little Dipper handle and can be confused with the Big Dipper. Prevent confusion by using both the Big Dipper and Cassiopeia

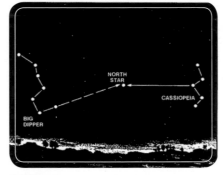

© US Army

together. The Big Dipper and Cassiopeia are always directly opposite each other and rotate counterclockwise around Polaris, with Polaris in the center. The Big Dipper is a seven-star constellation in the shape of a dipper. The two stars forming the outer lip of this dipper are the "pointer stars" because they point to the North Star. Mentally draw a line from the outer bottom star to the outer top star of the Big Dipper's bucket. Extend this line about five times the distance between the pointer stars. You will find the North Star along this line. Cassiopeia has five stars that form a shape like a "W" on its side. The North Star is straight out from Cassiopeia's center star. After locating the North Star, locate the North Pole or true north by drawing an imaginary line directly to the earth.

THE SOUTHERN SKY

Because there is no star bright enough to be easily recognized near the south celestial pole, a constellation known as the Southern Cross is used as a signpost to the south. The Southern Cross or Crux has five stars. Its four brightest stars form a cross that tilts to one side. The two stars that make up the cross's long axis are the pointer stars. To determine south, imag-

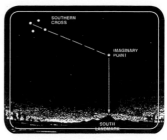

© US Army

ine a distance five times the distance between these stars and the point where this imaginary line ends is in the general direction of south. Look down to the horizon from this imaginary point and select a landmark to steer by. In a static survival situation, you can fix this location in daylight if you drive stakes in the ground at night to point the way.

OTHER MEANS OF DETERMINING DIRECTION

The old saying about using moss on a tree to indicate north is not accurate because moss grows completely around some trees. Actually, growth is lusher on the side of the tree facing south in the northern hemisphere and vice versa in the southern hemisphere.

If there are several felled trees around for comparison, look at the stumps. Growth is more vigorous on the side toward the equator and the tree growth rings will be more widely spaced. On the other hand, the tree growth rings will be closer together on the side toward the poles.

Wind direction may be helpful in some instances when there are prevailing directions, and you know what they are.

Recognizing the differences between vegetation and moisture patterns on north- and south-facing slopes can aid in determining direction. In the northern hemisphere, north-facing slopes receive less sun than south-facing slopes and are therefore cooler and damper. In the summer, north-facing slopes retain patches of snow. In the winter, the trees and open areas on south-facing slopes are the first to lose their snow, and ground snowpack is shallower.

MAKE A TERRAIN MODEL

If you find yourself in a survival scenario where you are required to hole up in a stationary position for an extended period of time, it will suit you well to build a terrain model which is simply a model representing the terrain in and around your hole-up site. This will help you to become better acquainted with the area and will mitigate your chances of getting lost as you venture out on foot. It will also help keep you oriented to where your rescue signal fires are located in the event that you need to light them in a hurry and their locations are not readily visible to the eye.

PONCHO RAFT

You may find when navigating through the wilderness that a water crossing is unavoidable. Since water often leads to civilization, using it to navigate to safety may be prudent in a survival situation. In any case, you will want a flotation device whether you are a strong swimmer or not. It is also advisable to waterproof your clothing and equipment, if possible. To make a poncho raft, place your gear along with some natural or man-made floating materials such as dried brush into the center of your poncho, then sinch it up tight and tie it off at the top or roll your contents up in the poncho, then tie it off at both ends. **Warning:** Take particular caution to currents, undercurrents, and cold water temperatures, as all can be deadly. Always continue to assess risk and only take risks when the benefit greatly outweighs the risks involved.

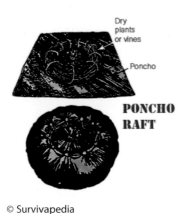

Dry plants or vines

Poncho

PONCHO RAFT

1. Equipement on poncho

2. Poncho rolled with pigtails

3 Second poncho being rolled

4. Pulling and pushing raft

© Survivapedia

© Survivapedia

Firecraft

© Brian Morris

Disclaimer: Please use caution when working with fire and flammable/combustible materials that can lead to personal harm, injury, and/or death.

ire is a beautiful thing. It can treat water, cook meat, sterilize, cauterize, provide lifesaving heat, and light up the darkest night. Our mastery of this element is one of the things that separate us from our primate cousins. Yet, for most of us, without a lighter or matches, fire-starting might as well be alien technology, because the ability to produce it on demand is not a skill set most people have any longer.

> When Green Berets are at a pause for training or combat operations, they make fires to sit around and shoot the sh*t and discuss the following day's plans. This time by the fire is a good way to reenergize yourself, raise your morale and mental outlook, and prepare you for taking on another day of keeping yourself and those with you alive.

What is fire? It seems simple enough: It's just a concoction of heat, oxygen, and fuel. So, why did it take humans so long to master it, and why is it that even today, most humans still have no idea how to produce it in the absence of a mechanical instrument? Well, to begin with, the conditions to make fire have to be just right or it simply won't happen. Anyone who has ever tried to master the bow drill or the pump drill can tell you that. In this chapter, you will find all the techniques and instructions needed to give you the greatest chance to build on your firecraft skill set.

BASIC FIRE PRINCIPLES

Understanding the concept of the fire triangle is very important in correctly constructing and maintaining a fire. Fuel (in a nongaseous state) does not burn directly. When you apply heat to a fuel, it produces a gas. This gas, combined with oxygen in the air, burns. The three sides of the triangle represent air, heat, and fuel. If you remove any of these, the fire will go out. The correct ratio of these components is very important for a fire to burn at its greatest capability.

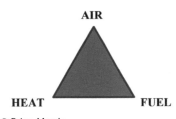

© Brian Morris

SITE SELECTION AND PREPARATION

You will have to decide what site and arrangement to use. Before building a fire, first consider:

- The area (terrain and climate) in which you are operating.
- The materials and tools available.
- How much time you have.
- Why you need a fire.

Look for a dry spot that:
- Is protected from the wind.
- Is suitably placed in relation to your shelter (if any).
- Will concentrate heat in the direction you desire.
- Has a supply of wood or other fuel available.

MATERIALS NEEDED TO BUILD A FIRE

You need three types of materials to build a fire: tinder, kindling, and fuel.

Tinder: Tinder is dry material that ignites with little heat. A spark starts a fire, so tinder must be absolutely dry to be sure just a spark will ignite it. Small, dry fibers, small twigs, and other materials that are small and thin enough to ignite quickly are all good examples of tinder. **Tip:** Make a feather stick by finding a dry, sturdy twig and shaving slivers around it, leaving the shavings connected to the stick at their base. The thin shavings will ignite much more easily than the unshaven stick itself would.

© Brian Morris

A great way to expedite the building of a fire is to replace traditional tinder with a solid fuel fire starter that can be purchased and prepacked into your survival or fire-starting kit. Combustible solid fuel will greatly increase your chances of getting a fire started under adverse conditions.

© Brian Morris

© Brian Morris

Put dryer lint into your survival or fire kit, as it makes for outstanding tinder.

If you happen to come across a bird's nest, save it and try to keep it dry. Birds' nests make outstanding tinder and provide you with a place to drop a burning ember as you begin to establish a fire. This is particularly important when making a friction fire, as the ember you initially create may be small and your time to get it to ignite into a flame will be limited.

How to Make Char Cloth

If you only have a device that generates sparks, charred cloth will be almost essential. It holds a spark for long periods, allowing you to put tinder on the hot area to generate a small flame. You can make charred cloth by heating cotton cloth in a tin container with ventilation until it turns black but does not burn. Once it is black, you must keep it in an airtight container to keep it dry. Prepare this cloth well in advance of any survival situation if possible. Add it to your individual survival kit. **Caution:** Do not put airtight tin or metal containers on a fire, as they may explode and cause harm or death. Make sure the tin you make your char cloth in is ventilated.

© Brian Morris

Kindling: Kindling is readily combustible material that you add to burning tinder. This material should be absolutely dry to ensure rapid burning. Kindling increases the fire's temperature so that it will ignite less combustible material. Small branches of dead tree are good examples of kindling.

Fuel: Fuel is less combustible material that burns slowly and steadily once ignited. Logs and other large pieces of wood are good examples of fuel.

Lighter knot, aka fat wood, is easy to find anywhere you can find pine trees. Look for the resin-saturated hard wooden core of rotted out pine trees.

© Brian Morris

SELECTING YOUR SITE

If you are in a wooded or brush-covered area, clear the brush and scrape the surface soil from the spot you have selected. Clear a circle at least one meter in diameter so that there is little chance of the fire spreading. Use rocks to build a retention wall all around the edge of the cleared area.

FIRE WALL

If time allows, construct a fire wall using logs or rocks. This wall will help direct the heat where you want it. It will also reduce flying sparks and cut down on the amount of wind blowing into the fire. However, you will need enough wind to keep the fire burning.

© Survivapedia

Caution: Do not use wet or porous rocks to build your fire containment walls, as they may explode when heated.

DAKOTA FIRE HOLE

In some situations, you may find that an underground fireplace will best meet your needs. It conceals the fire and serves well for cooking food. To make an underground fireplace or Dakota fire hole:

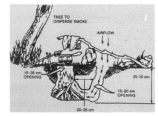

© US Army

- Dig a hole in the ground.
- On the upwind side of this hole, poke or dig a large connecting hole for ventilation.
- Build your fire in the hole as illustrated.

FIRE BASE

If you are in a snow-covered area, use green logs to make a dry base for your fire. Trees with wrist-sized trunks are easily broken in extreme cold. Cut or break several green logs and lay them side by side on top of the snow. Add one or two more layers. Lay the top layer of logs opposite those below it.

© Brian Morris

FIRE-STARTING TOOLS AND TECHNIQUES

There are several methods for laying a fire and each has advantages but the situation you find yourself in will determine which fire to use. The single most important step to having a fire is the ability to start a fire. The following are examples of techniques that you can use to start a fire.

LIGHTER

Anyone who ventures into the wilderness without a lighter is simply asking for trouble. A lighter is an amazing technology that people often take for granted. One small lighter can offer you thousands of ignitions, and the lighter's ability to create a spark can continue to benefit you long after the lighter

© Brian Morris

has run out of fuel. A good technique to ensure you always have a lighter on you is to tape a 550-cord lanyard onto your lighter, then loop a small carabiner onto the free-running end of the lanyard. You can even go a step further and put ten to twenty wraps of electrical tape or strips of °Gorilla Tape around the lighter so that you always have tape to use in an emergency. You can even start a fire with an empty lighter by either igniting char cloth with the sparks from the empty lighter or by slowly grinding the wheel of the lighter onto a piece of paper until a pile of flint dust accumulates. Carefully place a small pile of tinder on top of the flint dust, then use the spark created by the lighter to ignite the flint dust which will in turn ignite the tinder. Quickly place the burning tinder into your birds' nest or larger pile of tinder and gently blow on the pile until it ignites into flame.

Tip: If you want to add more functionality, you can add several feet of monofilament string and thin binding wire to your setup by looping them tightly around the outside of the lighter, then securing in place with a thin strip of tape.

GUNPOWDER

To access gunpowder in a cartridge, the bullet must be pulled. The projectile is typically crimped in place and the strength of the crimp depends on the type and caliber of cartridge. Use a Leatherman-like multi-tool to wiggle out the projectile from the shell casing or a sharp knife to cut through the plastic shotgun shell casing to get to the precious gunpowder located inside.

© Brian Morris

When ignited, gunpowder will reach over eight hundred degrees and burn for several seconds, maximizing your chances of igniting your tinder and getting it hot enough to ignite the kindling and fuel. Fire could truly be the difference between life and death and is also a *huge* morale booster.

Caution: *Do not* shoot yourself!

FLARE

Keeping a flare in your EDC is a good idea. Keeping two flares is an even better idea. When it comes to being able to start a fire quickly and with relative ease, it is hard to beat a flare. This is particularly true in times of emergency when hypothermic conditions have placed making

fire at the top of your survival priorities. To start a fire with a flare, simply set up your fire, taking the fire triangle into account, then use the flare to ignite the fire. Make sure that there is plenty of space for oxygen flow and ample amounts of the driest kindling and fuel that you can find.

FRICTION FIRE

Friction fires are without a doubt the most difficult fires to obtain because they mandate a great deal of skill and energy to produce.

HAND DRILL

The "simplest" method for making a fire via friction in dry climates is the hand drill. The concept is simple: cut a V-shaped notch into a soft, pithy piece of wood, which will be your fireboard, use a rock/knife or whatever you have at your disposal to make a small depression adjacent to the notch, then place a bit of bark  under the notch. Dust from the fireboard will build up into an ember, which will eventually begin to emit a faint wisp of smoke. Next, put the spindle (a pointed hardwood stick) in the depression and rotate it vigorously, rolling it between the palms of your hands while applying downward pressure. As the harder spindle rotates in the softer baseboard, it drills into it, creating friction and heat in the process. Once the hot dust forms a coal, you will see a wisp of smoke that can be delicately applied to your tinder bundle and blown into flame.

BOW DRILL

This method involves using a little bow for rolling the spindle and is far more efficient than doing it with your hands only. Using a strong stick and some string, fashion a small bow, leaving enough slack in the string to loop the string around the spindle portion of the drill. Place a rock with  a divot or depression the size of the diameter of the spindle stick on top of the stick and with the opposite hand begin to methodically push and pull on the bow which will in turn spin the spindle and create friction.

OTHER FIRE-STARTING METHODS

FIRE PLOW TECHNIQUE

The fire plow technique is straightforward. Cut a groove in a soft piece of wood, which will be the fireboard for all intents and purposes, then rub/plow the tip of a harder shaft up and down the groove. This technique produces its own tinder, as the sticks rubbed together will push out tiny particles of wood ahead of the friction. Continue to plow in a smooth, methodical fashion until smoke and a small ember is produced. Quickly place the burning ember onto your larger tinder pile and begin to gently blow on the ember until it sets your tinder into flame.

© Survivapedia

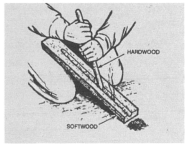

© Survivapedia

MAGNESIUM BLOCK OR BAR

Magnesium, when shaved down into thin flakes, will ignite and burn at extremely high temperatures of about 4,000°F. One magnesium bar will last a very long time, providing ignition for potentially thousands of fires. While most metals will corrode over time, magnesium will not (except when used in or near salt water), making it an excellent piece of gear to keep with your equipment when venturing into the wild. They are also extremely light and most come with a chain to connect to your kit. Additionally, most magnesium bars are set with a ferrocerium rod attached so all you need is a hard steel striker, if your bar did not come with one. Most magnesium bars have no handle, making them difficult to handle and shave. Consider shaving your magnesium bar beforehand and storing the shaved flakes in a plastic baggie in your fire kit. Shave the magnesium flakes onto the sticky side of a piece of duct tape to keep them from blowing away on a windy day or falling through the gaps in your kindling bundle or bird's nest. Magnesium flakes are the easiest to ignite when the magnesium is piled together and the spark is less than four inches away.

> **Tip:** Instead of wearing down the sharp edge of your knife by using it as a striker, break or cut off a 3" piece of jigsaw blade and keep it in your kit with your magnesium bar to use as a striker.

FERROCERIUM ROD (AKA FIRE STEEL)

A ferrocerium rod is made from a mixture of magnesium and several other metals called misch metal. These rods light fast and their sparks burn more than twice as hot as a match. You can get a ferrocerium rod to spark in virtually any weather and one single rod can provide a survivor with the sparks to ignite thousands of fires. These rods are virtually indestructible, but they can corrode over time. Look for ferrocerium rods made of high carbon steel. A good tip for getting the best spark from a ferrocerium rod is to hold the striker stationary in one hand and the rod up against the striker with your other hand. Pull back, applying upward pressure to the striker with the hand holding the ferrocerium rod. The hand holding the striker should not move. This will cause a ball of sparks to be thrown down and forward toward your tinder pile or bird's nest.

> **Tip:** Paint your ferrocerium rod with model paint or nail polish to extend its shelf life during periods of long-term storage. Use turpentine or paint thinner to remove the paint before use.

FIRE PISTON

The fire piston works under the principle that air gets very hot when compressed at high pressure. When you compress air inside a fire piston, it happens so quickly and efficiently that it can instantly ignite a piece of tinder placed at the end of the piston. Ancient methods of making fire pistons involve using hardwood or even a horn for the tube. The tube must be closed at one end, accurately bored, and very smooth inside. The gasket can be improvised from fiber or leather to create a seal for the piston to get the compression required. It is not a bad idea to keep a fire piston in your EDC pack.

FLINT AND STEEL

If you strike a softer steel against flint (which is harder), you'll produce sparks to ignite fire. You can also make fire in the same way with flint, marcasite, pyrite, fungus, grass/leaf, and quartzite. Since this method will only produce a spark and not a flame, you will need to use it with something like char cloth or another material that will ignite with only a spark.

BATTERY AND GUM WRAPPER

To use this technique, you will need a foil gum wrapper and any small cylindrical battery. Start by cutting down the wrapper so that the center of the wrapper is about ¼ width of the ends. Place one end of the wrapper on the positive end of the battery and the other end of the wrapper on the negative end of the battery. Be ready, as this will cause the wrapper to immediately catch fire. You want to be prepared to ignite your tinder pile immediately. Make sure you are protected from the wind when using this technique, as you may only have one chance and the tin and paper wrapper will burn quickly and could easily be blown out by the wind. Variations of this method include using a D battery and a thin copper wire from inside of something like a cell phone charging cable or by touching steel wool to a 9-volt battery.

JUMPER CABLE AND CAR BATTERY

Emergency and survival situations often start with a disabled vehicle. If you find yourself in a situation where you need a fire and you have access to a car battery and some jumper cables, attach one end of the cables to the positive and negative leads on the car battery. Next, tap together the positive and negative free-running ends of the jumper cables to create a large spark. If you do this over a pile of dry tinder, it should ignite quite easily.

Caution: Remove the battery from the vehicle and move a safe distance away from the vehicle to the location you plan to build your fire, as having a fire in such close proximity to your vehicle could cause the vehicle to set fire and make a bad situation even worse.

MAGNIFYING GLASS

It is smart to include a small magnifying glass in your survival kit. To make a fire with a magnifying glass, simply hold it at an angle over your tinder pile to allow a beam of magnified sunlight to concentrate on a pinhead-sized portion of your tinder. Keep the light in the same location on the tinder pile as best you can. The tinder should begin to smoke at the point where the light is concentrating down on it. You can then begin to gently blow on the tinder pile until it ignites into a flame. Variations of this technique include using a condom or plastic bag filled with water or urine to create magnification through light refraction. You can also try using a lens from glasses or even a chunk of ice. While these variations are viable, they are not by any means easy and require practice and a certain degree of luck.

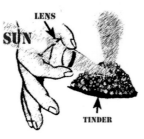

© Survivapedia

FLASHLIGHT

To start a fire with a flashlight, start by removing the lens and taking out the reflective cone that seats the light bulb. Next, place a small amount of tinder such as dried moss into the center of the cone. Place the cone in direct sunlight. As the light is reflected inward towards the tinder, it will cause the tinder to ignite or at least smoke into a workable ember. Be prepared to drop the burning ember onto a larger tinder pile and blow on the tinder pile until it ignites into flame.

FIRE IN A WET ENVIRONMENT

Starting a fire in adverse weather such as wind and rain is a very important survival skill that anyone who considers themselves to be an "outdoorsman" should possess. The ability of igniting a fire when things are less than perfect is a fine art which must be learned and practiced until mastery is achieved. The thing is, nature doesn't care much about our best laid plans, mice and men alike, and an emergency never comes alone. I mean, when confronted with a survival situation, you'd at least expect fine weather, cool breezes and sunshine. In reality, your survival in an emergency situation will become much more complicated than initially thought and I would dare to say nine times out of ten, as you'll end up not only lost in the woods or wherever, but you'll also have to deal with rain, cold and high winds. Emergencies almost always 'bring' bad weather with them. Think of it as a two for one deal. And that's fine as long you're prepared both physically and mentally. However, in critical times, your survival may depend on your ability to light a fire under rain and/or wind. Carry a full PACE plan of 4 separate tools for starting a fire. The idea is that a regular fire starter may not always provide you with the best results, especially if it's raining and wet. If it's windy and rainy, your chances of igniting a fire with just one match and cold hands are slim. In freezing cold and at high altitude standard BIC® lighters (which use butane) work poorly and eventually will not work at all.

STARTING FIRE IN THE SNOW

Knowing how to start a fire in the snow may save your life someday. Wintertime is arguably the hardest in terms of outdoor survival and if you can't build a fire you are going to freeze, regardless of the gear you have at your disposal. As night falls, the temperature will often plummet, making you feel

like you're in an icebox. If you can't make a fire, you may find yourself in a life-threatening situation. In addition to keeping you from freezing to death, fire keeps wild animals away and allows you to cook (or defrost) your food, and even make water by melting snow or ice. Fire is your best friend when it comes to wilderness survival, as it takes care of all that's important for a survivor: food, water, and shelter (warmth).

CHOOSE THE RIGHT SPOT

Selecting a proper site is the first thing to consider and is exceptionally important for your success. The location should ideally be protected from wind, water, and snow. Most folks traveling outdoors during the winter prefer to make a fire under a tree to avoid snowfall. This can backfire if the tree is carrying a lot of snow on its branches, as the snow may fall into your fire as it melts and put it out. If you're going to start your fire under a tree, make sure you knock the snow off the branches first. That eliminates the aforementioned risk and will also make sure you don't have to clear your spot twice.

BUILD A FIRE PLATFORM

Snow will melt at some point and the water may quench your hard work along with the flames, so construct a fire platform to keep your fire up off the snow. Even a sheet of heavy-duty aluminum foil from your pocket survival kit will work. You can also construct a platform out of sticks, logs, or rocks as long as it is dry or covered with dry material. You can build

© Brian Morris

a fire directly on snow or ice if you construct a platform first. Clear the snow by brushing it away or you may walk on it to tamp it down. If you're going for the tamping, you must realize that the snow will melt at some point, so make sure the water resulting from melted snow can drain away from your fire. Raising the combustible materials just one or two inches above the ground will make all the difference in the world by offering the water its required drainage channels.

WOOD STORAGE

Remember to clear the snow off the ground on a place near the fire for storing your extra wood and, if possible, try to use rocks for raising your wood storage spot above the ground. It would be ideal to use a large, flat stone as the fire floor but if you don't have enough rocks you can use sticks laid cross-wise or make a platform using branches (the same can be used for the fireplace itself in case you can't find rocks). Both ways are good for keeping wood from making contact with the ground, thus offering it the chance to get as dry as possible before use.

© Brian Morris

BUILD A REFLECTOR

Starting a fire in the snow is all about keeping you warm, and a good heat reflector is aimed at accomplishing exactly that. A big tree or a large rock makes for a good heat reflector. You can always improvise one from a blanket, the silver survival types, using the silver side which will provide you with the best reflection.

STARTING A FIRE IN INCLEMENT WEATHER

Just as in any wilderness fire, the first things you want to have to start a fire in inclement weather are tinder, kindling, and fuel. If you don't have tinder already stored in your EDC, you can always use small pieces of dry wood which are usually easy to spot near the trunk of trees. If you can't find small dry pieces of wood, get your knife, find the driest dead branch possible, and

© Brian Morris

whittle down until you hit dry wood. Carve that into feather sticks. If you don't even have a knife because of some freakish happenstance, break flint, chert, volcanic glass, glass, or quartz-based rock until you end up with a flake that will cut, and you are back in business. Avoid wood that was in contact with the snow, as it will have high moisture content. The same rules apply to kindling and wood for fuel.

© Brian Morris

Tip: A packet of waterproof matches and a couple of BIC® butane lighters are a must-have item in any survival kit. Ideally, you should also carry a dedicated fire-starter kit, which consists of a paraffin candle, magnesium block or bar, ferrocerium rod, ceramic or carbide scraper, medical cotton, and white petrolatum. **Note:** Carry the medical cotton and white petrolatum separately. Their uses are unlimited . . . until you mix them.

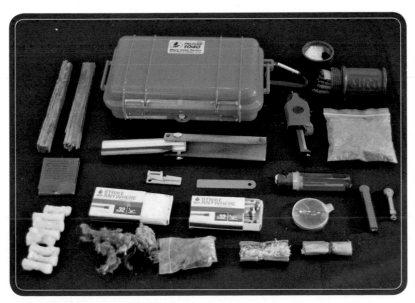

© Brian Morris

Bola

The bola is a field-expedient tool that is easy to make and is especially effective for capturing running game or low-flying fowl in a flock. To make a bola, simply tie a rock to a two-foot rope. Repeat this two more times. Once you have three lines with rocks secured to the ends, take up all three free running ends of the lines and tie them into a knot. To use the bola, hold it by the center knot and twirl it above your head. Release the knot so that the bola flies toward your target. When you release the bola, the weighted cords will separate. These cords will wrap around and immobilize the fowl or animal that you hit.

1 Use overhand knot to join three 60-cm cords.

2 Tie 0.25 kg weight securely to ends of cords.

3 Hold by center knot and twirl the bola over your head. Release toward target.

© US Army

Improvised Tools and Equipment

Green Berets know the importance of keeping a knife on their person at all times. A knife is your most valuable tool in a survival situation. Imagine being in a survival situation without any tools or equipment except your knife. It could happen! You might even be without a knife. You would probably feel helpless, but with the proper knowledge and skills, you can easily improvise needed items. In survival situations, you may have to fashion any number and type of field-expedient tools and equipment to survive. Examples of tools and equipment that could make your life much easier are ropes, rucksacks, clothes, nets, ant fd so on.

BASIC KNOTS AND LASHINGS

Before you start making tools, it will first help to become familiar with the use of some basic knots and lashings that can help you in the process of constructing tools that will last and hold together when needed most.

If you are prepared, you will most certainly have a long length of 550 paracord with you in your EDC pack. Having some sort of synthetic cordage in an emergency or survival scenario will offer the survivor a plethora of options no matter what the survival needs or task. If you have no cordage and you have nothing on your person or that is part of your clothing or equipment that can be repurposed as cordage, you can make your own from

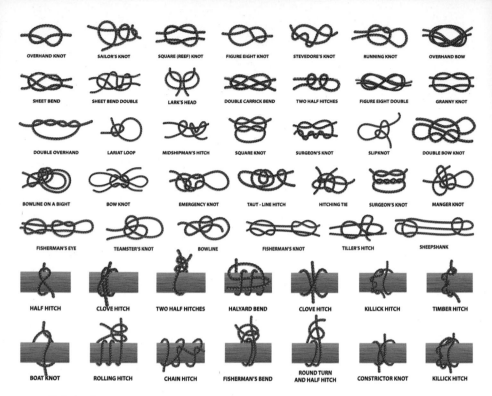

Basic knots

natural materials that can be found in the wilderness such as plants and/or animal carcasses.

The best natural material for lashing small objects is sinew. You can make sinew from the tendons of large game, such as deer. Remove the tendons from the game and dry them completely. Smash the dried tendons so that they separate into fibers. Moisten the fibers and twist them into a continuous strand. If you need stronger lashing material, you can braid the strands. When you use sinew for small lashings, you do not need knots, as the moistened sinew is sticky and hardens when dry.

You can also shred and braid plant fibers from the inner bark of some trees to make cord. Use linden, elm, hickory, white oak, mulberry, chestnut, and red and white cedar trees. After you make the cord, test it to be sure it is strong enough for your purpose. You can make these materials stronger by braiding several strands together.

You can use rawhide for larger lashing jobs. Make rawhide from the skins of medium or large game. After skinning the animal, remove any excess fat and any pieces of meat from the skin. Dry the skin completely. You do not need to remove hair from the skin or stretch the skin if there are no folds to trap moisture. Cut the skin while it is dry. Soak the rawhide for two to four hours or until it is soft. Use it wet, stretching it as much as possible while applying it. It will be strong and durable when it dries.

IMPROVISED TOOLS AND EQUIPMENT

SIMPLE HAMMER
A rock that is large enough to strike down on an object to bore it into the earth, crush, or crack open objects and small enough to be held in your hand will work well as a hammer.

PINE BOUGH SNOWSHOES
You can use a pine bough as a snowshoe by tying the bough to the bottom of your shoe. The bough will increase the surface area that your weight is distributed on, helping you walk on snow without sinking all the way down to your groin, depending on the snow depth.

SHOES AND GLOVES
You can use animal hides and other natural materials to fashion hats, gloves, shoes, or shoe covers for your head, hands, and feet. Remember that in cold temperatures your head, hands, and feet will get cold the fastest, as they lose heat more quickly than the rest of your body. Because of this, it is important that if you find yourself in a survival situation without the proper clothing, use what is around you to protect yourself from the elements. If you are near the remains of an aircraft or a disabled vehicle, do not overlook the raw materials that can be salvaged to help construct clothing and equipment to keep you alive.

BACKPACK
If you are prepared, you should already have your EDC pack with you, but that may not always be the case. Additionally, you may need to fashion a different type of pack that will allow you to move natural materials more easily from one place to another, as could be necessary when constructing shelter or when building a fire. You can use reeds or other natural or man-made material to fashion a backpack. You want to construct a pack that will help you to evenly distribute the weight of your gear and not cause severe chafing to your skin when loaded on your back.

CLOTHING/BLANKETS

If you do not have the appropriate clothing or sleeping gear with you, you may need to make your own from whatever man-made or natural materials are available to you. Even if you do have something like a sleeping bag or survival blanket, you may need to reinforce it with insulating materials such as the foam from inside seat cushions or natural materials like pine needles, straw, grass, and leaves. You can also make clothing out of the fur hides of dead animal carcasses. This technique is not easy, and it is time consuming, but it can be done.

Bushcraft Cooking: Prep, Cook, and Preserve

Caution: To kill parasites, thoroughly cook all wild game, freshwater fish, clams, mussels, snails, crawfish, and scavenger birds. Saltwater fish may be eaten raw.

FOOD PREPARATION AND COOKING

HOW TO PREPARE AND COOK MAMMALS AND BIRDS

The process of preparing and cooking mammals and birds is quite similar. Generally, hands, feet, and head are removed. Next, an incision is made down the center of the belly side of the animal from the neck down to the anus which will expose all the animal's organs. Being careful not to rupture anything, remove the guts from the animal. Now, remove the skin by peeling it down and away or leave the skin on for added flavor from the fat under the animal's skin.

> **Tip:** In an extreme cold survival scenario, as an absolute last resort you can use a large mammal carcass such as an elk, moose, or bear to transfer its heat to your body. To do so, you must first dispatch the animal if not already dead, then cut an incision down from its neck to its anus. Remove enough guts to make room for your body, then enter into the animal's chest cavity. The inside of a recently dispatched mammal can keep you warm for hours after its death.

> **Fun fact:** A three-ounce squirrel offers about one hundred calories and eighteen grams of protein!

HOW TO PREPARE AND COOK FISH, REPTILES, AND AMPHIBIANS

FISH

Preparing fish in a survival scenario is a bit different than it would be in most American households. The biggest differentiating factor is the level of waste. In a survival situation, no part of the animal should ever go to waste. Even parts that you do not plan to eat such as the guts,

scales, fins, cartilage, etc. can be used as bait with your traps and snares. Bones can be used as intricate tools or even turned into fishhooks. The fish flesh itself is in most cases safe to eat raw (saltwater fish only), or you can smoke it, dry it in the sun, or cook it on a fire on a hot rock or skewer. Fish skin generally contains a large amount of fat that you can either eat or separate for other uses. Larger fish should have scales scraped off prior to eating. Tiny fish can be cooked and eaten whole. To prepare a fish for eating, scale (if necessary) and gut the fish soon after it is caught. Insert your knife point into the anus of fish and cut open the center of the belly. Remove all its entrails.

Tip: Remove gills to prevent spoilage.

HOW TO PREPARE AND COOK NUTS AND PLANTS

If you are certain that the nuts and plants you plan to cook are of the edible variety, they can be an extremely nutritious addition to your survival diet. Nuts provide protein and fat. Most edible nuts and plants can be eaten raw and you can keep many essential vitamins and minerals intact if you do so. Some greens can  taste bitter, so cooking is a way to get rid of the bitterness and make it more palatable to taste.

Tip: Plants and nuts can be added to meats to cut through the gamey flavor.

Danger: Do not assume that you can cook away the toxicity of a nut or plant. If not 100 percent certain of the identity of a nut or plant, *do not eat!* If it's an emergency survival situation, *take caution* and use the universal edibility test (see on page 33).

HOW TO PREPARE AND COOK CRUSTACEANS AND MOLLUSKS

In a survival situation, you would be fortunate in an area where mollusks and crustaceans are plentiful. As long as you are able to cook them properly and identify the ones to avoid, you can add a lot of nutrients to your diet by including these shellfish. The follow-  ing crustaceans and mollusks are safe to eat with a few exceptions (see next page for more information about dangerous crustaceans and mollusks):

CRUSTACEANS
Crab, crayfish (crawfish), lobster (coral), prawns, shrimp

MOLLUSKS
Abalone, clam, cockle, conch, limpets, mussels, octopus, oysters, periwinkle, quahaugs, scallops, squid (calamari), whelks, geoducks

You should cook crustaceans and mollusks thoroughly by either boiling them or roasting them over a fire. You can also steam them. **Note:** Crustacean and mollusk allergies predominantly affect adults and are less common among young children. These allergies tend to develop later in life than the common childhood allergies. Allergies to crustaceans and mollusks are usually lifelong conditions.

> **Caution:** Eating raw crustaceans and mollusks can be dangerous. These animals may harbor bacteria that can be harmful to your health. If you are not certain that the animal is free of toxins, you should cook it to well done or boil it for three to five minutes before consumption or avoid them altogether as a survival food if possible.

HOW TO PREPARE AND COOK FROGS, SNAKES, TURTLES, AND LIZARDS

FROGS

Some frogs are poisonous so if you are not certain of the species you should avoid them as a survival food, but most frogs can be eaten if identified and prepared properly. Using a bushcraft gig or a makeshift net is your best bet to capture these creatures in a survival scenario. It is easiest at night with a flashlight fixed directly on the frog to keep the animal from seeing you. Frogs are most active at night and can be found near water sources such as lakes, ponds, and streams. Once caught, start by killing the animal. This can be problematic, as they are notoriously resilient creatures. Use a rock to bash in the frog's brains or throw it at a tree or large rock at a high rate of speed to kill the animal. Most of the meat on a frog is in its hind legs. Use a knife to cut through the tough skin around the waist of the animal. Cut off the feet on the frog's hind legs. Next, use the pliers on your multi-tool to peel the skin off the frog's hind legs as if taking off its pants. Once the lower portion of skin is removed, cut off the hind legs from the rest of the frog's body and cut them in two. Use the rest of the body and skin as bait for trapping or fishing.

> **Caution:** Colorful frogs are usually toxic and should be avoided as a survival food. Never eat frog skin, as it can also be toxic.

SNAKES

All snakes are edible if prepared properly. Even venomous snakes can be eaten, but you must use extreme caution and remove the head and venom sacks before preparing or eating. To kill a snake, you should pin down its head with a stick that is "Y'ed" off at the end, then quickly dispatch the animal by cutting off its head. The next step is to remove the snake's skin from its body by cutting an incision from its anus all the way up its belly to the top of the creature where its head used to be. Now, pull the skin downward, peeling it completely off the animal. Remove all the guts from the inner cavity of the snake and dice the meat into chunks to be cooked well-done on skewers over a fire or boiled in a stew. You can also wrap the snake around a green stick like a rotisserie and then roast it over a fire until the meat is well done.

Danger: Poisonous snakes can deliver a deadly bite long after the animal has been killed, so use extreme caution when handling these animals, dead or alive. You must cut the snake's head off three to six inches below the head to ensure you have removed the venom from the animal. Use extreme caution when discarding the head by burying it as deep as possible and then covering it with a large rock to prevent it from being dug up.

TURTLES

These animals can be difficult to kill and will continue to move long after their head is removed. The best meat on a turtle is on their legs and their necks. You can use their shells to cook in or eat out of and use the rest of their body as bait. To prepare a turtle, remove the plate on the underbelly of the animal. Remove the legs and thighs for consumption. Remove the neck for consumption. Cook the meat well-done to ensure you destroy all dangerous bacteria such as salmonella. Wash hands thoroughly after having contact with turtles.

Caution: Some turtles such as the American Snapping Turtle can be quite dangerous and could easily sever a finger or toe if you are not careful. The best way to handle these animals is by holding them upside down by their tail.

LIZARDS

When it comes to alligators and crocodiles as a food source, smaller is better. Adult alligators and crocodiles can easily take down and kill an unwitting adult human, so avoid them as a survival food source. Baby and juvenile crocs and gators are far less likely to eat you before you eat them and they are relatively easy to catch with bait, net, or hook and lure, but their bites can be extremely painful and cause injury, so caution should be taken when handling them. Take care not to be injured by their claws, tails, or most of all their teeth. Small lizards can be eaten whole by skewering them and cooking them over a fire. Prepare a larger lizard in the same fashion as you would small mammals, by removing the skin and thoroughly gutting the animal before cooking. Lizards are edible, like all reptiles, but they carry dangerous bacteria so should be cooked thoroughly. Cook lizard meat well-done to ensure you destroy all dangerous bacteria such as salmonella. Wash hands thoroughly after having contact with lizards.

> **Caution:** If you are in an area with baby crocs or gators, it is always a possibility that mom is in the area, so take extreme caution when you find yourself in a survival scenario where these animals are present.

HOW TO PREPARE AND COOK SNAILS AND SLUGS

Snails: Most garden variety snails are edible, but some are poisonous to humans, so if you do not know what you are looking for you should avoid them as a survival food source. If you are going to eat a snail you should cook it thoroughly first by either roasting it on a skewer or boiling it for three to five minutes.

Caution: Some snails are toxic and should be avoided as a survival food unless you can 100 percent identify them as an edible species. All sea snails should be avoided, as they contain the most venom of all slugs and some can potentially kill humans if handled or consumed.

Slugs: While slugs are edible, they can be toxic if they feed on toxic plants or mushrooms, so they should be avoided as a food source in a survival scenario.

HOW TO PREPARE AND COOK INSECTS, WORMS, AND ARACHNIDS

Most insects, worms, and arachnids can be eaten raw or cooked. Insects often have a pleasant nutty flavor, and cooking will greatly improve their taste. This is particularly true when roasted. Most of the nutrients you want are in their abdomen section so remove the wings, barbed legs, and heads of insects and arachnids prior to cooking. **Tip:** Drop worms into potable water for at least thirty minutes. They will naturally purge themselves of all waste, significantly improving their taste.

The easiest way to cook insects, worms, or arachnids, once you have removed their nonedible parts, is to use the skewer method. Start by running a sharpened twig through one or several of the critters' bodies like a shish kebab. Once you have them skewered, take the bottom ends of the skewers and implant them into the ground at about a 45-degree angle over the hot coals of a fire. Let them cook crisp, turning them until done.

Caution: Insects with a hard outer shell have parasites and should be cooked before eating.

FOOD PRESERVATION

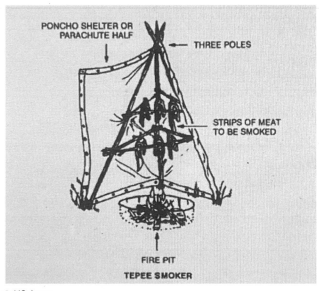

© US Army

FREEZING

Food buried in snow maintains a temperature of approximately 32°F. Frozen food will not decompose. **Tip**: Freeze in meal-size portions. Food wrapped in waterproof material and placed in a stream remains cool in summer months. Earth below the surface, particularly in shady areas or along streams, is cooler than the surface.

SMOKING

To smoke meat for preservation, hang it one to two inches over a hot burning fire and add green wood to create smoke. The heat of the fire and the smoke will cook the meat and it will create a tough outer layer that will help preserve the food for later consumption. *Do not* use pitch woods such as fir or pine because they produce soot that will give the meat an undesirable taste.

DRYING

Meat and fruit can be dried in the sun until all the moisture is removed. This will extend the shelf life of the food. The thinner you can slice the food, the quicker and more thoroughly it will dry in the sun.

SALTING

Salting meat will help extract the moisture and prolong shelf life.

APPENDIX

Survival Use of Trees

F ew wilderness survival resources are more important than trees, so making camp in proximity to trees makes a great deal of sense, as it puts the survivor's shelter in proximity to resources and often provides a solid support structure off which to build. Trees can also provide areas to build a shelter that are relatively free from deep snow. In these cases, trees can save a great deal of time and work. Saving work by building off what is already provided by nature burns fewer calories and helps keep the survivor from working up a sweat, which can lead to severe discomfort or put the survivor at risk of hypothermia in cold weather.

- Trees mean shelter from cold and heat alike. Some species of trees indicate the presence of surface water and any good campsite has an inexhaustible supply of firewood, so make for the trees.
- Most hominid apes, including humans, build nests. Our ancestors have been building nests in trees for a long time, so you could say it is in our DNA.

TREES PROVIDE MANY IMPORTANT SURVIVAL RESOURCES

- **Fire:** Trees can provide tools and tinder to start fires and fuel to keep them going.
- **Shelter:** Boughs provide insulation from the cold, hard ground. Branches and leaves provide a roof. Trunks and branches provide structural support, a windbreak, and insulation.
- **Safety:** Trees provide concealment and large trees can provide cover or a refuge from predators, snakes, thorns, and biting insects.

Branches from thorny trees or shrubs can also be used to create a barricade against predators.

- **Water:** Some species of trees provide drinkable water or provide support and shade for water-bearing vines. Trees also provide materials to treat water by boiling.
- **Cordage:** Bark is an important source of cordage material.
- **Food:** Many species of trees produce edible nuts, fruits, leaves, or layers of bark. Forests, trees, and transition zones along the borders of forests or stands of trees provide key habitats for many animal species. Trees also provide engines to power snares and traps, can channel game to traps, and provide secure anchor points for traps, nets, and bank lines for fishing.
- **Medicine:** Many species of trees have medical uses.
- **Tanning:** Branches are useful for frames to stretch hides and the bark of some species is useful for bark-tanning hides.
- **Tools and weapons:** Trees provide materials for fishing hooks, bows, arrows, spears, clubs, battle hammers and axes, and other important tools and weapons.
- **Communication:** Trees are useful for some methods of short-range communication, making trail signs, and for blazes.
- **Navigation:** Trees can be useful in direction finding and ascertaining the direction of prevailing winds when choosing campsites.

TYPES OF TREES

While there are many species of trees, they can generally be broken down into two categories, deciduous and evergreen.

DECIDUOUS TREES

Deciduous trees tend to lose all their leaves for part of the year. In colder climates, this happens in autumn and the trees remain bare through the winter. In hot and dry climates, deciduous trees usually lose their leaves during the dry season. Many deciduous trees provide nuts and fruits which make them an outstanding resource.

You can also use their branches for a plethora of survival applications, as described above and below.

EVERGREEN TREES

Evergreen trees are excellent to have as an available resource in a bush-craft survival scenario because they tend to keep all their leaves through-out the year. The leaves of evergreen trees have many uses. You can use the green boughs as fuel for signal fires, as the live branches tend to create a lot

of smoke. You can make shelter from the boughs and leaves. You can even eat just about everything on a pine tree, from making tea from its needles to eating its bark in an emergency situation.

TREE SHELTER DANGERS

Survival requires a certain degree of risk management. Since there are a few dangers inherent to tree shelters, they should be weighed against other dangers before making the call to invest the energy and take the risk of building a shelter in a tree. Following are some of the dangers that trees can present.

WIDOW MAKERS

Widow makers are dead branches or treetops. They are so called because high and heavy enough specimens sometimes inflict fatal wounds.

CRITTERS

Trees should be inspected thoroughly for venomous arthropods, snakes, and other potential threats/opportunities. Should you be so lucky as to find scorpions in your potential shelter, you just found some grub. Cut off their tails, roast them, and pop the "land shrimp" in your mouth. If you find a snake, you will have a better meal.

FALLING

Falling even a couple of feet and hitting your head on a sharp rock makes a bad survival situation even worse. If the hardware holding your hammock gives way, you could just end up bruised and embarrassed, but you could also end up with skull fracture and a traumatic brain injury, depending on how you land. So, if you are thinking about saving a couple of bucks by purchasing carabiners stamped "Not for Climbing Use," you might want to rethink.

RESPIRATORY DANGERS

Any tree that looks like it has the makings of a home probably looked like a home to many animals that found it before you did. Unlike most humans, many species of animals urinate and defecate where they sleep. This creates more of a danger than just foul smell, especially in dry climates and when bats are doing the defecating. Bat droppings are easily kicked up as dust and breathed into the lungs, where they can cause respiratory illness.

FIRE

As with any debris shelter, fire is always a danger, but when you combine that with the fact that you are up a tree where your mobility is limited and you are liable to fall, fire becomes even more dangerous. Outside a very narrow range of circumstances, keep your fire on the ground.

CAMOUFLAGE

Debris shelters are notoriously difficult to spot since they are basically hunting blinds that blend perfectly with the environment. If you want to be found, be sure to construct signals where they can be seen before you hole up or your chance to be found may stroll right on past.

About the Author

© AnnMarie Mello-Morris

Brian M. Morris is a retired US Army Special Forces Master Sergeant who served on active duty for more than twenty-five years. He is a decorated combat veteran and a specialist in Survival, Evasion, Resistance, and Escape (SERE) training.